Riding the Rollercoaster of Life.

Riding the Rollercoaster of Life.

Living with Bipolar/Manic Depression.

Luann Punke Rimpel

XULON PRESS

Xulon Press
2301 Lucien Way #415
Maitland, FL 32751
407.339.4217
www.xulonpress.com

Paperback ISBN-13: 978-1-6628-3502-5
Ebook ISBN-13: 978-1-6628-3503-2

"May the words of my mouth and the meditation of my heart be pleasing in your sight, O Lord, my Rock and my Redeemer."
(Psalm 19:14 NIV)

Dedicated to:

My Savior Jesus Christ who promised,
"Lo, I am with you always, even unto the very end of the world."
(Matthew 28:20 KJV)

My husband, who has been faithful in good times and bad,
up times and down times,
and who kept reminding me that,
"Greater is he that is in you, than he that is in the world."
(1 John 4:4 KJV)

And finally to:
My pastor, counselor, confidante and friend, who spent countless
hours pointing me to the cross and drawing out the motive in my
heart for my behavior. "A motive in a man's heart is like deep waters,
and a person who has understanding draws it [the motive] out."
(Proverbs 20:5 NET)

Table of Contents

Special thanks to Sarah,
who holds a Master of Science in Psychology,
and without whom this project
would never have come to completion.

Special thanks also to my son, Joshua,
for putting my compositions into print form.

And finally, special thanks
for the many prayers of my faithful prayer warriors.
God bless you all!

To My Beloved Husband

Tim is such a simple name
That it would really be a shame
Were you to seek for worldly wealth
To bring some fame upon yourself.

But as I view your life I see
It's just the way that it should be
A life of serving Christ your Lord
Living according to His Word.

The righteous man is blessed of God
Such blessing promised in His Word
I see this as I gaze upon
Our precious daughter and our son.

Because of this I can't express
How very great the happiness
That I have found in serving you---
A mother, wife and sweetheart too!

Our love will grow through toil and woe
At times the tears may have to flow
But there are also times of joy
Our love has grown: A girl! A boy!

And as we grow in Christ our Lord
We find we simply can't afford
To spend our time in arguing
Or other grievous sinful things.

For if we spent our time in such
We'd see that we would lose so much.
Such things would Satan use to smother
Our growing love for one another.

So often when at home I'm one
(It seems your work is never done)
I thank and praise our God above
For giving me your steadfast love.

And so, dear Timothy, I pray
To Jesus Christ our Lord each day
That He would keep us in His care,
Protect us from the devil's snare,
And teach us truly how to share
The love we for each other bear.

My love I give with all my heart
A love you kindled from the start
And when we from this life shall part
May we a life in heaven start
With Christ on high
After we die
There to be
Eternally

**Love,
Luann**

To My Pastor:

My pastor prayed for a sister, but he got daughters instead. I prayed for someone, who could help me through my emotional health struggles, and I got much more than I could have ever imagined. He won my heart when he told me I could call him "collect" if I was ever in trouble.

After years of counseling sessions and serving together at church, along with my doctor's care, my health has stabilized to where, today, I manage my household and juggle three part time jobs, all while struggling with a major mental illness. I do my best to, "Always be prepared to give an answer to everyone who asks [me] to give the reason for the hope that [I] have." (1 Peter 3:15 NIV) As for my husband, I love him more dearly as each day goes by!!

Introduction

Jesus is all-sufficient, no matter what the need. His ways are not our ways, so sometimes we won't understand, and perhaps we will not understand what He allows in our lives until we get to heaven. Daily time spent with Jesus is of utmost importance in this life on earth.

If you struggle with a mental illness, I want to encourage you to try to make use of all options available. I found that medication alone was not sufficient. I also found that nutrition alone was not sufficient. The results of my "experiments" were often unpleasant, to say the least.

I also found that medication and nutrition together were not sufficient. I needed other people. I sought the help of doctors - including psychiatrists, counselors - including my pastors, and also many friends. My support group has been phenomenal over the 40 plus years of struggling with my psychiatric label.

It is my prayer that my book provides encouragement where encouragement is needed and comfort where comfort is needed, with the understanding that my book does not even hold a close second to "God's Big Book," the Bible.

Chronicle

Before I Was Diagnosed

I was born in September, 1957, the fifth child in a family of seven. My father was a telephone man. Sometimes he climbed telephone poles, and later he had an office job. My mother was a stay-at-home mom, and she didn't drive, so she was limited to having someone get her places. She was a fine seamstress and did many other crafts as well.

We grew up in a modest home that my parents built in Brookfield, a suburb of Milwaukee, WI. There was always food to eat; my mom cooked to feed a crew. For the most part, we had a happy childhood. My parents argued quite a bit, but I never thought we'd be anything but a family.

My parents felt one of the best ways to educate us was to take us traveling all over the US. I believe I was in every one of the continental states. I have a "patch jean jacket" that my little sister sewed for me in college. I sewed my patches on by hand, since I had no sewing machine. After my mom's death, at 66 years of age in 1991, I inherited all her patches, so I made another "patch jacket."

Most of our trips were to Florida over Easter or Christmas, but twice we went out West for a whole month. We also went out East. They always chose a different route, so we could drive through more states, even if only a corner of them. We camped in a trailer. Our first trailer was a wooden box that we put poles up and threw canvas over. We had to snap all around it. Our record time to set this up was 15 minutes. That was eventually replaced by a pop-up camper. Luxury!!

I was very anxious to go to school like my brothers and sisters. Since my birthday was past the deadline, I had to be tested to see if I was ready.

The only thing I remember about the test was being asked what was missing from the shoe. The answer: the shoe lace. Easy! The only thing I remember about Kindergarten was that we had mats to take our nap on. For Kindergarten and 1st grade I attended public school. The rest of grade school I went to our WELS Lutheran school.

I did well in school, but I had to work hard. My brothers, on the other hand, had it easier. I did, however, graduate 8th grade as valedictorian. I attended Wisconsin Lutheran High School in Milwaukee, and did well academically there too. This time two of us tied at the top of our class. Our GPA was 96.51. As co-valedictorians, we both prepared a speech to deliver at graduation. That was in 1975.

Then in spring of 1976, as a college freshman at Dr. Martin Luther College, I lost my mind!

Double Diagnosis

Today, I am diagnosed as bi-polar/manic-depressive. I had one manic episode at the end of my freshman year in college and spent the month of May 1976 in a mental hospital. I was able to complete the classes I missed in the summer and returned to college in fall to find out I was officially a sophomore. Since 1983, I have been under the care of a psychiatrist. For almost a year, in 1991, I was under the care of a medical doctor who studied nutrition and was advising me to lower my meds and take supplements. When I thought I was pregnant, I was advised to stop all meds. A manic episode resulted and I was "forced" to go back to my psychiatrist, who does not believe in nutritional supplementation.

As a little girl, I was terribly afraid of the dark and of any natural disaster. In my last year of high school, at times, I felt like I was walking through a fog, like I was lost, and I was very confused. As a freshman in college, experiencing my first crush, I felt I had a vision of heaven when I was in the 3rd grade, where I had walked and talked with Jesus. I was hospitalized for one month and given valium. I finished college, married and had two children. My youngest was almost a year old when I felt I needed to go and witness of Christ to my entire town by myself. I was

2

hospitalized for two weeks (November 1983) and given lithium and stelazine. When I drank spiked punch at a wedding reception, I was hospitalized again for two weeks (June 1984). That Christmas (1984), I was admitted to a hospital that no longer exists, under the care of a Christian psychiatrist and a Christian psychologist. After three months of intensive psychotherapy, our insurance ran out, and I was transferred to a state hospital. After two weeks, I returned home, and I was a MESS! I came home the first day of spring in 1985.

Then a friend of mine shared information about a nutrition center in Naperville. They analyze hair, blood and urine and do a heavy metal screening. Their lab work is an analysis of your body's bio-chemistry. When I went, I had a routine physical. A nurse checked all my vital signs and proceeded to cut a handful of my hair. I consulted with a doctor for about an hour. I had to wait two weeks for my test results. I was told that the best thing I could do was flunk one of the tests, for then they could do something to help me.

I did flunk one of the tests! I received five pages of test results. I was awed at what they had to tell me. I was told I had a genetic stress disease called PYROLURIA. Everyone's body has molecules called kryptopyrroles. They are made with the hemoglobin and are passed out with the urine. My urinalysis showed that my body has very many of them. As they pass out, they leech me of B-6 and zinc, both which I need to cope with stress. A healthy count would be 4.5; a person would exhibit symptoms with a count in the teens or twenties; a child who complains to mom that he can't behave in school and doesn't know why, might have a count of thirty. My count was 59.4. I was seriously ill with this genetic disease. But of all the bio-chemical diseases of this nature, mine was the easiest to cure.

The nurse mentioned several symptoms of pyroluria: inner tension, low self-esteem as you see yourself overact in the presence of others, inability to perform well at school, in boys-behavior problems, aggression, hyperactivity, inability to handle stressful situations, incorrect perception of what is stressful, depression, mood swings, fatigue, headaches, in general, a wearing and tearing on one's body.

Everything made sense, except that I did get good grades. I was told I also have high histamine, which is a neuro-transmitter stored in the basophils (blood cells). High histamine enabled me to achieve in the midst of very difficult circumstances. But along with high histamine comes depression, foggy thinking, compulsiveness and an inability to turn off negative thoughts or feelings.

Physically, I was healthy. No anemia, no infection, no diabetes, kidneys and electrolytes fine, liver good, body proteins good, low on choles-terol due to mal-absorbing my food (nutrients), no sign of gout, HDL cholesterol great, thyroid good--all indicated by blood and urine tests. The hair analysis indicated toxic minerals, lead and cadmium, were fine. Calcium, magnesium and zinc were excreted in my hair and needed to be replaced. High calcium, high magnesium, low manganese and low chromium indicated borderline hypoglycemia. And high sodium indi-cated above-average intelligence!

I bought 16 bottles of supplements to empty in three months. These supplements were designed specifically to treat my illness.

8/19/92	kryptopyrrole	59.42	histamine	70
12/29/92	"	22.37	"	54
8/12	"	2.69	"	25

Comments: 2.69 is an excellent count for the kryptopyrroles, but 25 is a little low for histamine.

Luann's History
Where do I begin?

BIG SIGH!!

I noticed some confusion of my thoughts in high school and wasn't sure I could be a teacher. I attended Wisconsin Lutheran, a large Lutheran high school, and I remember walking down the halls being unsure of which door to enter. I remember that I forgot to go to my organ lesson a couple times. I loved my organ lessons! But my guidance counselor told me I would be fine. That's it! I was told my good grades proved that. So I did go to Dr. Martin Luther College in New Ulm, MN, and began my training to be a Christian day school teacher. It was in May of 1976 at the end of my freshman year at DMLC that I experienced my first break from reality. The precursor to this break was several nights of little or no sleep. I had my first manic episode and thought that I had received a vision from heaven. I thought Jesus had sent me on a special mission on earth. I spoke in my third grade voice as I thought back to my favorite teacher and her class. My teacher's daughter was actually at school with me, and, at the suggestion of her mother, she took me on a walk up a hill at the park in New Ulm, and asked me to walk up the hill barefoot. The point being made was that I was still on earth. My parents picked me up and I was admitted to a hospital in Wisconsin. I was hospitalized for one month and given valium. I did not receive a psychiatric label at this time. I was able to finish the final quarter of school during the summer and received a notice that I actually was a sophomore shortly after the school year started.

Things were pretty stable, considering my bouncy personality, which is far from steady, and I graduated from college in 1979. I married my husband, Tim, who had graduated from DMLC the previous year. I taught Vacation Bible School during what I thought was going to be the second week of my honeymoon, and then I taught 1st grade for most of the year. I only taught until Easter, because my dream to be a mother became a reality: Joshua Timothy was born on May 3rd, 1980.

When Joshy was a year and a half, I was asked to teach Kindergarten, for a half day. My pastor's wife babysat. I walked to school and cried the whole way, six blocks or so, because I was leaving my son behind. I loved teaching; it was just hard to leave Josh behind. I got pregnant again with Rebekah Ann, who was born on November 11th, 1982. So, both years I taught, I was pregnant. That was hard for me.

Then things really started to "go wacky!" On a nice fall day in October of 1983, when Becky was only 11 months old, I had another manic episode. I dropped my children off at my neighbor's house, dressed in "clash-day" clothes, and went for a walk with my puppy, wearing no shoes. I was hospitalized for two weeks and labeled Bi-polar. I received lithium and an antipsychotic medication. I was told to have "no alcohol, not even one drop." That was no problem since I don't drink anyway… The summer of 1984 I drank some spiked punch at my friend's wedding and had another episode. I knew the punch was spiked, but since I'd already had a swallow, I just drank the rest of my glass. This time I was very mean to Tim. At this point, I was taking lithium and stelazine.

That same winter of 1984, I was hospitalized from just before Christmas until spring of 1985. For these three months, I received intensive psychotherapy from a Christian psychologist and a Christian psychiatrist. The hospital I was at no longer exists. When our insurance ran out, I was transferred to a state mental hospital in Tinley Park. Two weeks later, on the first day of spring, I was released and I was a MESS! At this point, the psychologist turned me over to the psychiatrist, feeling I only needed help managing my medication.

I tried to concentrate on good eating habits, exercise, drinking lots of good water, Scripture memory and taking nutritional supplements.

In 1990, a friend introduced me to Calli cleansing tea, which I began using. I also saw a nutritional family doctor in Highland, IL. He worked with me from September of 1990 to August of 1991. On December 14, 1990, I was struggling and called my pastor for help. He encouraged me to call my husband, Tim, who was coaching a game in Michigan. I told him to come home right away. He came home FURIOUS! He brought his mom to "keep the peace." The doctor I was seeing in Highland weaned me off my medication, but I was taking halcyon to sleep. We took a vacation to Interlocken, a very prestigious music camp, and I was fine the whole time. But when we got back, my psychiatrist put me on 20 mg of stelazine - the highest dose I'd had.

My mother died in October 1991. She was a great loss to so many! She was only 66 years old.

At some point in 1992, I began to see Ruth as my counselor. She was very kind and helped me a tremendous amount. Ruth only charged what I felt I could afford. In September, I started a supplement program from a nutrition center. I was diagnosed there with a stress disease. I also made a phone call to the president of our seminary in Mequon, WI, to ask why they wouldn't accept my husband as a student! (Tim is a great theologian, but I think our seminary felt he couldn't handle the languages required. Tim was advised to study some Greek, which he did with our pastor's help.) In November that year, my psychiatrist lowered my tranquilizer more than ever before. A school bus rear ended me when I was driving my daughter to the library; there were Thanksgiving, Christmas and New Year's celebrations and I was fine through all of this. My maternal grandmother died on New Year's Eve, though I felt that I had lost her years before this, when she no longer recognized me.

Sometime in 1993, I was taken off stelazine by my psychiatrist, but I don't remember if it was replaced with another medication. My checkup from the nutrition center showed much progress. My stress disease is one of the easiest to fix! In April, at the urging of my pastor, I appeared before the elders of our church with a "laundry list" of my husband's wrongs!! In short, he didn't lose his job. (See 1 Corinthians 13)

I tried melatonin, a natural sleep aid, which I started in 1994. My favorite type is the minty sublingual ones. I was exhausted from caring about and helping two single pregnant friends. One of my dear friends helped me quilt a baby quilt for each of them, quilts my little sister had sewed.

In January of 1995, five tests indicated that I was pregnant. On January 31, the OB/GYN matter-of-factly declared that I had miscarried. (I wrote a diary to "Isaac", my baby that I lost, which is included in this book later.) I think this might be when our insurance changed, and I had to switch psychiatrists. No more trips to Skokie in tons of traffic.

In 1996, I lost five key people in my support system due to relocation to another state. The hardest for me to lose was my pastor. Much earlier in our relationship, he told me about "transference", where a person being counseled can feel like they are "falling in love" with their counselor. He told me not to worry and that he would make sure nothing happened. I was so relieved to hear that and anxious to tell Tim. Tim was VERY UNHAPPY and told me I better be CAREFUL!! The next thing I remember is writing a letter to my pastor and being called into his office with Tim and having my pastor scream at me about trying to "ruin his ministry." I think he gave me a big bear hug when I left his office with Tim. I was reeling and totally mixed up. As we left, I heard him tell my friend that I was going to be fine. I don't remember when that happened. But I do remember that the next letter I wrote to him was when he received a divine call to California, and I told him that I thought I could manage without him if he left Crete. I prayed for every word I wrote.

I was mourning the loss of my friends when I went to Camp BASIC in June of 1997 and ended up having a manic episode there. I don't remember much about it, just that I didn't go back to Camp for a very long time. Tim and I saw a counselor from September 1997 through March 1998. I kept hoping someone would tell Tim how to improve.

We had another counselor in 1999, but he billed us under my name instead of Tim's, so I quit and Tim was happy about that decision.

After this, I was stable for a long time. For a while I tried to take vitamins from my friend, but it proved to be much easier to get my supplements from the Center that was treating me. They are able to make a compound especially for my body chemistry.

2002 was a very interesting year. While teaching more than 20 students at school and more than 20 students at home, I became pregnant. I found out right away and stopped my medication at the direction of my psychiatrist. This time, my baby lived!

Jacob Josiah was due on my mother's and grandmother's birthdays, June 26. He was taken by C-section at 29 weeks because I had pre-eclampsia. The doctor had to take him on April 14 to save my life and his. He only weighed 1 ¾ pounds (seven sticks of butter) and was 12 ¼" long. He was in the NICU at Rush in downtown Chicago for three months. He has Down syndrome. I waited almost as long as Abraham waited for Isaac, but I wasn't even waiting anymore. My psychiatrist told us my pregnancy was probably the best thing that could have happened to me, but that after our baby was born, my symptoms would come back with a vengeance. I did have to go back on my medication, but I was still able to nurse Jacob. I nursed him for a LONG time. After all, there weren't going to be any more!

My father died in October of 2009. He is dearly missed.

In 2015, my psychiatrist had a real problem with my mail-order pharmacy and was in failing health, so I switched to another psychiatrist for a short time until I was told my insurance wasn't paying him. I'm not sure exactly when, but I now have a female psychiatrist and I really like her. I do not like virtual visits!!

July 1, 2020, was when I started using only Juice Plus products. I actually make a commission on the products I purchase, and I love the products! Now in 2021, I also take a few supplements from the nutrition center and a few things from Shaklee too. The biggest problem I have consistently is struggling to fall asleep. My psychiatrist claims I don't have a sleep problem, but she did prescribe hydroxyzine to help on nights like tonight when I'm on my chromebook or another device too late.

Comment: I was born in 1957 and graduated in 1975. I celebrated my golden birthday when I turned 12 because my birthday is September 12th. I celebrated my golden birthday again in 2014 because I turned 57 years old and I was born in 1957. My sisters and I couldn't figure out how that worked. I wish my dad was here to help! He always liked numbers.

Important People

The TEAM: Pastor/Husband/Psychiatrist

Pastor--troubleshooter in town, fields calls from concerned, visited me wherever I was, *friend, counselor for me and at times with my husband

Husband--*faithful, committed spouse, provider, daily contact, discouraged over large cost of maintaining my health, not very attentive to me, quality time mostly at his convenience

Psychiatrist--*manage meds, extra contact when in trouble (usually when Pastor or my husband said so), returned calls faithfully and efficiently

*reason why each is most important to me

CONTEMPLATIONS

Favorite Proverbs

"A motive in a man's heart is like deep waters, and a person who has understanding draws it [the motive] out." (Proverbs 20:5 NET)

"Wounds made by a friend are intended to help, but an enemy's kisses are too much to bear." (Proverbs 27:6 NET)

"A friend always loves, and a brother is born to share trouble." (Proverbs 17:17 NET)

"A man and his friends can destroy one another, but there is a loving friend who sticks closer than a brother." (Proverbs 18:24 NET)

"A neighbor nearby is better than a brother far away." (Proverbs 27:10c NET)

"Do not set foot in your neighbor's house too often; otherwise, he will see too much of you and hate you." (Proverbs 25:17 NET)

"Now do this, my son, so that you may free yourself, because you have fallen into your neighbor's hands: Go, humble yourself and pester your neighbor; give no sleep to your eyes nor slumber to your eyelids; free yourself like a gazelle from the hand of the hunter and like a bird from the hand of a hunter." (Proverbs 6:3-5 NET)

Questions and Answers

From Pastor Donald Cole
(In Today in the Word Devotional)
Published by Moody Bible Institute
Used with permission

One month this question was asked: When I think about going to heaven, I am not always eager to get there. I am not in a hurry. Is this wrong?

Pastor Cole's answer: No, not necessarily. I am 74 but I'm in no hurry. I have many things still undone. Once we get to heaven, we'll be there a long time. Meanwhile, life is a "gracious gift" (1 Peter 3:7). The apostles made plans and lived fully until they were certain that they were about to be executed. Then they composed their souls for arrival in God's heavenly kingdom. Check this in 2 Timothy 4:6-8 and 2 Peter 1:13-15.

I was tickled to see he answered my question the very next month. My question was: Because I am usually depressed, I am eager to get to heaven. I don't want to deal with another day on earth. Is this wrong?

Pastor Cole's answer: The apostle Paul got the blues occasionally, which, admittedly, is not the same as clinical depression. I cannot speak for you, but I know how Paul handled his strong desire to die at times. When he was in prison he thought of other people and, knowing that his death would be a serious loss to them, he resolved to go on living, as much as it was up to him. His presence on earth was necessary for [them]" (Philippians 1:24). So he chose to stay alive (verses 20-26)

Most of us have things to do before we die (if only to pray for others), and, knowing that once we get there we'll be there a long time, we should be in no hurry to get there.

Suicide

A couple times at Bible class we've touched briefly on suicide, and invariably Dr. Kivorkian's name comes up. This is a difficult issue for me.

One who claims a person is foolish, as in ridiculous or absurd, for wanting to attempt suicide simply doesn't know what it's like. The truth is, it is foolish to a person in their right mind. A person in their right mind can't begin to comprehend the idea of taking or even desiring to take one's own life. If a person can't understand that desire, he/she can be very thankful.

To me, a person who would consider suicide has, so to speak, gone to a different "level of consciousness." Logical, rational thinking is not a part of the answer to the question, "Why am I here?" or "Of what use am I?" There are many factors that could lead one to this other "level of consciousness." When there is enough pain physically, psychologically, emotionally, or mentally, etc., one may choose to cope by ending his life. Suicide is a sin just like adultery or disrespect is a sin. It is a sinful way to cope with a present situation. I think suicide is a sin of impatience. "When God says to "wait on the LORD," (Isaiah 40:31) He means to wait. Suicide is playing God and trying to take into your hands matters that belong to God alone.

A dear friend, who lived in Michigan, said she thought Dr. Kivorkian used halcyon to encourage his patients to use his suicide machine. Halcyon is a sleeping pill. At one point I was taking halcyon every night for perhaps two weeks straight. Indeed, I did fall asleep, but I can't explain how horrible I felt when I woke up and realized I had to live another day! I believe taking halcyon could convince someone to use a suicide machine.

It is God's will that all should be saved. It is the devil's plan to destroy. Death is destruction. When I was praying, "God , let me die," Jesus interceded and the Holy Spirit interpreted my prayer to be, "Preserve my life." (Psalm 143:11, Psalm 119:37) "Let me live that I may praise you" is in Psalms 42 and 43 three times.

When I can't sleep, it gives me great comfort to know that God is awake. He never slumbers nor sleeps, but I must. He's God, I'm not. He watches over me yesterday, today and forever.

Almost every day I find comfort in Luke 22:31-32, substituting my name for Simon's. "Simon, Simon, Satan has asked to sift you as wheat. But I have prayed for you, Simon, that your faith may not fail. And when you have turned back, strengthen your brothers." NIV

Grieving

"Brothers, we do not want you to be ignorant about those who fall asleep, or to grieve like the rest of men, who have no hope." (1 Thessalonians 4:13 NIV)

Each person handles grief differently, and for me, it differed for each person I was grieving.

I lost my grandpa when I was only five years old. He and my grandma were in a car accident. My grandma broke her arm, but my grandpa went to heaven. I could not understand why God had taken my beloved Papa away.

When my mom left the Church Militant to join the Church Triumphant, I struggled. She was only 66 years old. I quit singing in the choir for a while. It was weird though; I remember lying on the couch in my basement and groaning from deep within as I thought about my dad joining my mom and leaving me behind. I grieved for them both at the same time.

When my grandma, my mom's mom, lost her mental health in a nursing home, I grieved for her. Years before this, she had been to our house in Illinois. I was pregnant with Becky. She stayed about a week. We baked donuts, just like she would do when she came to our house when I was a child, and just had a great time. I didn't see her often since she was in Wisconsin. At the end, she didn't even know who we were. So, when she entered the Church Triumphant, I could only rejoice. Nanny and Papa were finally together.

When my dad entered the Church Triumphant, I missed him dearly, as I had talked to him twice a week. But, as I already said, I had grieved his death when my mom died. The only thing to do was rejoice that his suffering was over. Now I talk to my little brother twice a week.

Then there's my nephew. He'd had no contact with his parents for a long time. I prayed so hard that he would be found. I had bought an elliptical bike with some of my dad's inheritance money. When his mom called to tell me my prayers were "sort-of" answered, she told me he had taken his life (suicide). I stopped using my bike and never got back to it!

When I was really sick (mentally unstable), I was not allowed to play for church for four years. I wept every time I went to church. My pastor said it was "too big of a step." Thanks to my little sister, I played for a service at her church in Indiana and did fine. I let "the church" know I was ready, but I still was not allowed to play. I couldn't play pre-service, post-service or offertory. Then there was a conflict and no one was able to play, so I was asked to play the whole service! Praise the Lord; it went well. God blessed.

I always wanted more children, but my psychiatrist kept saying, "No!" I grieved, more than I know how to express, the loss of more children. Proverbs 14:10 reads, "Each heart knows its own bitterness and no one else can share its joy." (NIV) I knew Jesus understood. In 1995, I miscarried at the early onset of my pregnancy. The diary I wrote to my baby, "Isaac", is included. But then, 21 years after Becky was born, we were blessed with Jacob Josiah. I was so ecstatic to read the positive pregnancy test! (for two seconds!!) Then it dawned on me that I'd have to tell Tim and I knew he wouldn't share my enthusiasm. I was so naive: no thought of diapers, lack of sleep, potty training... I just knew I had my heart's desire: another baby was on the way. My husband told me to tell NO ONE!! But I had to tell Caryl, my dear friend, who was so far away, and who loves babies as much as me. She told me to be sure to have my progesterone level checked, which I had to insist on, and it was in the large range.

I was almost 46 years old when Jacob was born. He was taken by C-section to save my life and his. Once he was here, I never thought we'd lose him.

He was in the NICU at Rush in Chicago for three months. He truly is our "million dollar, miracle" baby. The doctor had determined by ultra-sound that his umbilical cord was only going one way. As I see it, either he wasn't getting nourished, or he wasn't getting rid of waste. Either way, how is he here today? I had to wait almost as long as Abraham, and I wasn't even waiting anymore!

Finally, there's my pastor. Every time he's had health struggles with his heart or an ulcer, I would grieve as though I'd lost him. The first time I remember after he had had heart surgery, when he had returned home and was recovering, I was told he was at the band concert. I rushed over there to see him. I stood against the wall and scanned the audience. The band was playing "Beauty and the Beast." When he left, he walked past me and shook my hand. He was so weak; I needed the wall to hold me up.

When he took a Call to California in 1996, (Becky was going into 8th grade) I thought I'd never see him again. That was almost more than I could bear. His kids were like my own kids. His whole family was very dear to my heart.

A couple more times he struggled with his health and I thought I'd lose him for good. Each time I grieved the loss of a dear friend.

But he's still here today! God has been so good to me!!

Beverley Haar was the Dean of Women at Dr. Martin Luther College when I attended there in 1975 to 1979. She was my first counselor and was a tremendous help in getting me through my struggles in college by pointing me to God's Word. She was my dear friend in Christ. Following is a letter I wrote to her after Josh and Becky were born.

Dear Dean Haar,

CONTEMPLATIONS

There have been many times that I have wanted to sit down and write but too many things have had to take priority. Now, however, I am working on an assignment. Last Tuesday I went to see Ruth, a counselor from WLCFS, WELS. I have a Christian psychiatrist, but I was very unhappy with how he handled my last "crisis," as he called it. I am very much in need of someone I can call when I'm in a crisis. Often, my husband is unaware or not concerned. I believe my pastor is simply tired of my case. He has been such a blessing to me in the past, but for more reasons than I care to explain, he isn't really in the picture anymore. Since I am not happy with my psychiatrist and had such fond memories of our talks together, I asked about seeing a woman counselor. My husband and my pastor are not really for this idea and so it is with some apprehension that I seek Ruth's help. Our time together may be limited as she is to be replaced by one of my friends.

Anyway, I met with Ruth once and she asked me to try to remember some of the things we talked about and how you helped. I thought it might be easier if I was trying to write to you.

I can remember the first crisis that brought me to your door. My knees were shaking! I was uncertain about being a teacher since I didn't know if I loved God or He loved me. I think I even hated God for creating sex between men and women and I hated my mother for not telling me. My dream of being a mother was shattered. It was very traumatic to admit I had a problem. I'd never had anyone to talk with before. We discussed my dysfunctional family, perfectionistic parents and problems I faced in childhood.

The next crisis I remember was being unable to write a composition in Freshman Comp. I did well with this in high school. We worked through that and I think I got an A in the class.

I remember coming over to your house and having hot chocolate. I always had so many things to tell you and you were so willing to listen. I remember how you could find a Bible character to fit almost every problem I had. You'd say something like, "How do you suppose

17

(Daniel) felt? If God could take care of him, don't you think He can take care of this?"

Were you the one that used the illustration of a truck going down the road and leaving potholes? That is how we live our lives, but God comes and repaves the road. He keeps fixing our messes.

I really believe I was OK for seven years after my breakdown freshman year because I had you to come to for help. Now when I need help, they keep giving me more medicine and causing me more problems. I remember that first breakdown was over a crush I had, and he wasn't even interested in me. I didn't get over him until I met my husband. Then I felt guilty dumping him so fast! I had all kinds of struggles to face when I got back to school as a sophomore and you were there to help me through. Sometimes I just need someone to talk to or be with me.

Have they told you they diagnosed me as bi-polar/manic-depressive? Pastor says I'm schizophrenic. I just know I'm sick of being sick and there's not much hope of me being well ever.

Thank you for all the time you invested in my life. You have been a great blessing to me and are dearly loved.

Love,
Luann

Becoming a Mother

My heart's desire as a child was to be a mother. I was overjoyed with each of my pregnancies. When I was hospitalized for three months, from Christmas 1984 to the first day of spring 1985, I couldn't get better because they would not let me go back home to my kids.

I love my children more than I could ever say and have spent many hours in prayer for them, and now for their spouses and our grandchildren. I feel extremely blessed!

PRAYERS FOR KIDS (PFK's)

Genuine love for God	persevere in trouble
Desire to obey God	parental mistakes
Repentance in the light of sin	clothes and shoes
Desire to spread the Gospel	food and drink
Faithful study of God's Word	use of musical talent
Commit Scripture to memory	protection from strangers
Attend church faithfully	apply themselves at school
Freedom to worship	peer pressure
Health-physical, spiritual, mental, emotional	employment
Rock music, drugs, alcohol, smoking	good stewards of their money
Responsible with driver's license	protection from accidents
Adolescent, young adults, adults	virginity until married
Spouse that loves God, is faithful, a good companion, able to have kids Infants, toddlers, children	

Prayers for Tim and Me

Faithful	food and fresh water
Pray together	clean house
Time to talk	good health
Time to walk	study God's Word
Time to relax	be one flesh
Time to sleep	date nights

COMPOSITIONS

Songs I Composed

Music has always been a special part of my life. Following are some special songs I composed for different times and special occasions in my life.

Songs for Our Children

Joshua Timothy Rimpel

Josh is a little-bit-o' honey Josh is a honey-bun
I love that little bit-o' honey
He's my number one son!

Rebekah Ann Rimpel

Becky is a honey, She's a little snuggle-bunny
Smiles and coos to wipe away all your blues
She's so much fun she's our number one!

Jacob Josiah Rimpel

But I do, but I do, but I do, but I do
Love my little boy (Bubba-da-bump)
But I do, but I do, but I do, but I do
Love my little boy (Bubba-da-bump)
Oh, little boy, little "eedy", Oh, little boy little "eedy"
Oh, little boy, little "eedy"
Oh, baby boy! (Bubba-da-bump!)
(tune: Hallelujah)

Note: My mom encouraged all of us to try music. All of us were in band except my little brother, some longer than others. When I came home from church one day and started picking out the melody to "Hark the Voice of Jesus Crying" on our piano, she urged my dad to let us start piano lessons. My brothers and little sister didn't share my enthusiasm!

Jacob's song was a little harder since he wasn't a number one, but he was little for a very long time.

Josh and Becky's Songs

Luann Rimpel

1980, 1982

"Sing to [the LORD] a new song; play skillfully and shout for joy."
(Psalm 33:3 NIV)

Here Am I, Send Me! (Isaiah 6:8 NIV)

Here am I, send me, send me When I was a child you sought me.
I could hear you gently calling Never knew there'd be such falling
To your arms you sent me crawling Bringing me closer to Thee.
Though I am not always willing Faith in me you are instilling
In my heart your love is filling Teaching me to trust in Thee.
Here am I, send me, send me Use me till in Heaven I dwell with Thee.

Oh, dear Lord, I grieve within Every time I catch myself in sin.
That is when You keep assuring Constantly my faith securing
Helping me to keep enduring Finishing what I begin.
But, dear Lord, there's more that grieves me
Not till Heaven will it leave me
Saddened hearts are what displease me Christian bodies they are in.
For these children Lord I pray Teach them to rejoice in Thee alway.

Note: The melody for this song was composed my senior year at DMLC
in New Ulm, MN. I was very sad as Tim was far away in Crete, IL.
The words, however, didn't come until after my three month stay in a
mental hospital.

Here Am I Send Me

Luann Rimpel

2

Though I am not al - ways will - ing; Faith in me You are in -
But dear Lord there's more that grieves me; not till heav - en will it

still - ing. In my heart Your love is fill - ing; Teach - ing me to trust in
leave me. Sadd - ened hearts are what dis - please me. Chris - tian bod - ies they are

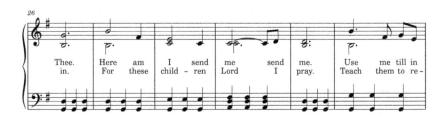

Thee. Here am I send me send me. Use me till in
in. For these child - ren Lord I pray. Teach them to re -

Heav'n I dwell with Thee.
joice in Thee al - way.

God is in Control
(for Pastor Lyon)

Luann Rimpel

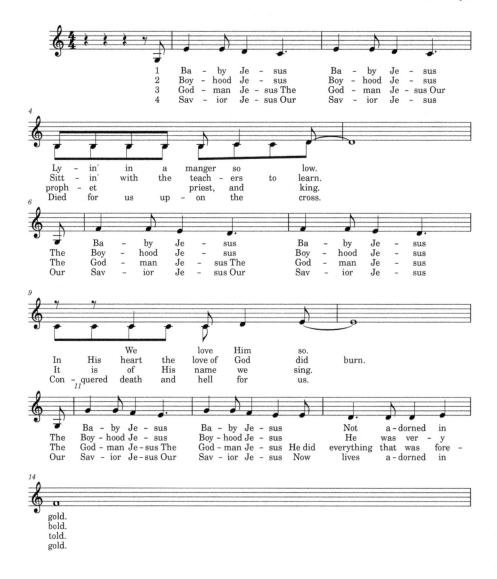

1 Ba - by Je - sus Ba - by Je - sus
2 Boy - hood Je - sus Boy - hood Je - sus
3 God - man Je - sus The God - man Je - sus Our
4 Sav - ior Je - sus Our Sav - ior Je - sus

Ly - in' in a manger so low.
Sitt - in' with the teach - ers to learn.
proph - et priest, and king.
Died for us up - on the cross.

Ba - by Je - sus Ba - by Je - sus
The Boy - hood Je - sus Boy - hood Je - sus
The God - man Je - sus The God - man Je - sus
Our Sav - ior Je - sus Our Sav - ior Je - sus

We love Him so.
In His heart the love of God did burn.
It is of His name we sing.
Con - quered death and hell for us.

Ba - by Je - sus Ba - by Je - sus Not a - dorned in
The Boy - hood Je - sus Boy - hood Je - sus He was ver - y
The God - man Je - sus The God - man Je - sus He did everything that was fore -
Our Sav - ior Je - sus Our Sav - ior Je - sus Now lives a - dorned in

gold.
bold.
told.
gold.

2

The	Ba - by Je - sus	Ba - by Je - sus	He was	in con - trol!	*To verse 2*
The	Boy - hood Je - sus	Boy-hood Je - sus	He was	in con - trol!	*To verse 3*
The	God - man Je - sus The	God-man Je - sus	He is	in con - trol!	*Chorus*
Our	Sav - ior Je - sus Our	Sav - ior Je - sus	He is	in con - trol!	*Chorus*

Chorus

Yes, God is in con - trol; Let me tell you God is in con - trol!

We should nev-er doubt or fear, for God is here to share our joys and our

tears. share our joys and wipe our tears through all of our

4 Our

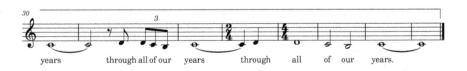

years through all of our years through all of our years.

GOD IS IN CONTROL! (Psalm 33:3)
For my pastor

Baby Jesus, Baby Jesus Lyin' in a manger so low
Baby Jesus, Baby Jesus We love Him so
Baby Jesus, Baby Jesus Not adorned in gold
Baby Jesus, Baby Jesus He was in control.

Boyhood Jesus, Boyhood Jesus Sittin' with the teachers to learn
Boyhood Jesus, Boyhood Jesus In His heart the love of God did burn
Boyhood Jesus, Boyhood Jesus He was very bold
Boyhood Jesus, Boyhood Jesus He was in control.

The God-man Jesus, the God-man Jesus Our Prophet, Priest and King
The God-man Jesus, the God-man Jesus It's of His name I sing
The God-man Jesus, the God-man Jesus He did everything that was
foretold The God-man Jesus, the God-man Jesus He is in control.

Yes, God is in control!
Let me tell you, God is in control!
We should never doubt or fear, for God is here
To share our joys and our tears...

Our Savior Jesus, our Savior Jesus Died for us upon the cross.
Our Savior Jesus, our Savior Jesus Conquered death and hell for us.
Our Savior Jesus, our Savior Jesus Now lives adorned in gold.
Our Savior Jesus, our Savior Jesus He is in control.

Yes, God is in control!
Let me tell you, God is in control!
We should never doubt or fear, for God is here
To share our joys and wipe our tears
Through all of our years,
Through all of our years,
Through all of our years.

Text and tune: Luann C. Rimpel
Christmas 1994

28

DIARY TO "ISAAC"

To "Isaac"
In loving memory

Sunday, January 22, 1995

Dear Baby,

Daddy and I just found out you're coming last Friday. I hope you can tell how excited I am to have you inside me. I have waited for you for so long! Your big brother, Josh, is almost 15 and your big sister, Becky, is almost a teenager. I think you'll be here before that happens, but I don't know yet.

Daddy and I are glad you happened but we're a little surprised and all. I'm a little scared because I kept taking my medicine even though I kind of thought you might be there.

As I think back, it seems you might have arrived on the scene with a trumpet fanfare. (I don't know how fast conception occurs.) Your dad and big brother played their trumpets in church-it was New Year's Day and they played Hornpipe. It was wonderful! And maybe you were there.
I don't know, but God does.

Today is my third day to not take my medicine and I'm a little jumpy. I don't think you mind, but it's a little hard on me. I think we'll get through it all right. But it's 9:59 and the lights are out at 10:00.

I love you, child.
Mom

_____

Tuesday, January 24, 1995

Dear Baby,

I wonder if you'll ever read this. I wanted you to know we went sledding at Goodenow Grove. I think you liked it. I did! I was a little scared, but I couldn't figure out how to tell Becky I wasn't going to go, so I went down the big hill and hoped for the best. I think we survived. Are you OK?

I am a little concerned about this spotting. I never had that with Josh or Becky. Besides, now that you're here, I don't know exactly where you'll be born, the doctors are still trying to decide. I don't care. I still say it was harder getting you "in the oven" than it will be to get you out! Perhaps Dad can explain that someday.

This is my 5th day to not take my medicine. I tremble sometimes, but my friend suggested that I read a Bible verse instead of taking a pill-to do it at the same time I would normally take my medicine. I'm going to try that today. Maybe you'll notice a difference??

I'm glad we're in this together for now. I hope we live through it. I have to go to work. Becky is my first student today.

Love,
Mom

———————

Wednesday, January 25, 1995

Dear Baby,

I guess you really are here. Do you want to know how God told me? Maybe someday you will, so I'll just write it now and you can read it later when you get big like Josh. He's a freshman at ILHS.

Will you play ball like your brother and sister do? What I really want to know is: will you play this extra organ I have in my kitchen? Your brother and sister don't seem interested and I had really hoped someone in the family would use it. Maybe that's why God sent you to Daddy and me.

Now what was I telling you? How did God tell me you are really here? My psychiatrist took me off all my medicine last Friday (1/22) because my neighbor had done two pregnancy tests. The first one was on Wednesday and it was inconclusive POSITIVE-there simply wasn't enough of you to be totally positive. You were totally POSITIVE when she repeated the test at the Pregnancy Counseling Center. So, that's the first I believed you were really here.

But then I started spotting and bleeding and I didn't know what to think. I remember telling God He could have you back, just in case He decided to take you right after He gave you to me. But then, I made an appointment, after that second test, with Homefirst. I had planned for so long-10 years?-that I would not go to the hospital to have any more babies, so you were to be my first attempt to deliver at home.

Do you know what the doctor said? He said we were High Risk! Look at that-not even three weeks old and we've got the same label. So will you be more Punke-like in vitality or more Rimpel-like? I don't care. I'll love you more and more as each day goes by.

Getting back to how I know you're really here. I was so upset about what the doctor said, calling us High Risk, that I forgot to ask him why I was spotting. So another day, I called him and he asked to talk to your father, but I had no idea where he was. I found him later and told him the doctor wanted to talk to him. Evidently Dad got a hold of him pretty quickly because in short order I was on the way to the hospital emergency room.

Becky stayed home with Sandy and Josh scored two points at his game. He played Varsity, but Mike scored most of the points that night. They lost because nobody else could "hit the bucket!"

Anyway, I wasn't really scared, I was just waiting to see what would happen. I took some things to read, "Smart Women Keep It Simple" by Annie Chapman, my Bible in a "lunchbox", and my God's Word to the Nations Proverbs, in case they kept me too long. We waited forever! I ate supper. Dad didn't, and we left for the emergency room. It was 1:30 a.m. when Dad crawled into bed to fall asleep and I slept a little because after all the testing and poking the doctor said, "The pregnancy is in the womb" (good! You're in the right place), "the cervix is tipped" (uh-oh, you're ready to come out?) and "the cervical os is closed" (but not yet!) He simply told me you were alive and I was not going to lose you yet. But I thought I already knew that and Dad didn't think he learned anything new either. But, I was more sure that God is in control of our lives, because even the nitty, gritty, finite details of our lives matter to Him.

I can't remember what else I wanted to tell you because I'm too tired. I have to rest, but first I'll check that buzzer on the dryer.

Hugs and kisses,
Mom

Thursday, January 26, 1995

Dear Baby,

I think my bleeding may stop in a couple weeks. I hope and pray it will so I can worry less and relax better.

It's not really your fault, but when God decided to use Daddy and me to make you, my hormones went goofy. That's why I started bleeding-because my hormones changed so quickly. But I never did bleed with Josh and Becky so I've been a little scared about you arriving safely in my arms. Now I should do better because Jesus tells me--

(Caryl, Mrs. B, just called to be happy with me that you are coming)

--that He has everything under control (Philippians), that I should not be afraid (Psalm 56:3) and that I should not worry-that sounds like Matthew and the Sermon on the Mount. Someday we'll talk about those special words in God's Book, but now Mommy has to eat something and rest.

I forgot to cancel my piano students' lessons today, so they came and I told their moms that you are coming in September, I think. Now they will pray for you to arrive safely too. Pretty neat, huh? But I'm going to ask your Dad if we can tell your big brother and sister because I don't want them to worry about me not doing some of the things I normally do, or grumble about helping me to do them. I can't wait to see their happy, surprised and excited faces! See, I already know them a little better than you do. But I will get to know you just as much; you'll see.

Hugs and kisses,
Your Mom

———————————

Dear Tim,

Please just let me share what Kay said about telling the kids.

First, she said if they were perceiving anything unusual or out of order and that we are keeping it a secret, we would not be building trust and would be asking them to ignore observations they are making.

Second, she said we need time to adjust before we tell them. So, can we please spend lots of time making adjustments so we can figure out the best way for us to tell them?

Third, if we share this privileged news and ask them to keep it quiet and not tell their friends, we are placing trust in their ability to do so. We are teaching them that we trust them and that they should feel free to trust us also.

Fourth, she said things may seem really obvious to us because we know what's going on, but others won't necessarily interpret what's going on in the same way.

She also said that kids now-a-days tend to immediately panic when they perceive things going awry because they fear divorce is pending. I don't believe our kids are panicking; I don't think Josh has much of an idea because he's been gone so much. I told Becky she was right in knowing that something was wrong, thanked her for caring and told her that when we figured out what was going on, we would be sure to let her know. Perhaps she could use your reassurance too.

Tim, I think this is a good time to thank God we made a pact and sealed it to never even mention the word "divorce" in our conversation. Let's renew that commitment. Kay keeps telling me we'll get through this.

Love,
Luann

―――――――

Friday, January 27, 1995 6:00 p.m.

Dear Isaac,

I have been really sick. Are you OK? My head aches, my throat has been sore and my chest tickles. I think I caught too many concentrated germs that night we spent at the emergency room, when we found out for sure that you were safe for now.

All day I tried to find a doctor to deliver you. I think, when the time comes, I should just carry around my knitting bag because I have scissors in it to cut your cord. (Don't worry; I've been advised against it!!)

I think we might tell your big brother and sister tonight. I think they'll be very surprised and very glad, but I don't think they'll want to share either of their rooms. You may have to sleep in Mom and Dad's room for a while. I know just where I'll put your crib (Becky slept in it too-right next to my side of the bed. I don't approve of you sleeping with Dad and me most of the time, but for the next eight months it'll be fine. But when you start making noise, you're out!

The truth is, I get really sick when I lose sleep. And one thing I remember about my other babies is that I lost sleep on occasion. But that's OK-now there are four of us to take turns all night. I'll handle the feeding part. Somebody else can walk the floor with you if you're not happy but everything else is taken care of, OK? I love you, Isaac. I have waited for you-it seems forever. Since Becky was born, I was planning on you being part of our family. Dad is adjusting day by day.

Keep growing, little one, so you're strong and healthy when it's time to be born and meet all of us. Dad says I think about you too much. But I can't help it. It seems like my bleeding has almost stopped already and I feel much less worried. Dad and I must still decide who will deliver you and where. And I'm thinking I might go to work Monday if God restores my health. At least you're not part of my health problem; you're the best thing that's happened to me in the past thirteen years, besides Dad. Eat, sleep and grow, kid!

Love,
Mom

Saturday, January 28, 1995 7:45 p.m.

Dear Isaac,

I am so tired! Can you tell I've been very busy today? I had to be at Becky's game this morning and watch her cheerleading, and Josh played on JV and Varsity for Homecoming, and I just don't know how I'll ever keep up with you too…but I can hardly wait to see you! Josh, Becky and me-we're pretty excited about you. Dad's given up hoping that you won't arrive and accepted the fact that you are coming and he's learning to love you more and more each day.

Know how I know? He prays with me for you and me every day. Look at that! Already you are competition. I have asked Dad to pray with me every day since we were married, but we must have been too busy, or whatever, and somewhere we forgot. But now that you've arrived on the scene, Dad and I are remembering to pray together. Aren't you special?!

Josh, Becky and I are wondering how big you are right now. I showed them my baby feet that are ten weeks old and you, if you're there yet, must be much smaller. But we're all hoping that you have two feet with five toes each, and that they're not too big! (Just kidding!)

Isaac, you make me so happy! That's why I called you Isaac for now, because it makes me laugh to think how God worked out the intimate details of your beginning: from popping a new song into my head to an error in charting and ignoring important variables, to you! Quite simple in God's plan, I guess.

We, (Becky and me), picked a name for you if you're a girl. How do you like the name Hannah Marie? The guys are supposed to come up with a guy's name, but for now Isaac will do.

My friends that know are praying for you and me, Isaac. Isn't that special? We probably won't tell any more people that you're coming until spring-that's March 21st. Maybe my family, my brothers and sisters will know by then if I get to see them-maybe not. Dad wants to wait until we have a better chance of having you arrive safely. That's after you've been growing for three months.

But, and I may be wrong, I just don't think God would take you away from me now, at least not until I can see you and hold you and touch you and kiss you.

I would be too sad. I love you, Isaac.
Mom

———————

Sunday, January 29, 1995 11:00 a.m.

Dear Heavenly Father,

I am struck with awe as I consider yet another factor that convinced me of what I already knew, that Isaac is no accident, but part of Your divine plan. You were there, when on New Year's Day, I was ready to play Hornpipe with Josh and Tim on trumpet. Could it be that Isaac was welcomed with a trumpet fanfare? Only you know how long it takes for conception to occur. Help us find the best place for Isaac to be born and clue us in on the name You already know for him. In Jesus' name,

Luann Carole Rimpel

———————

Monday, January 30, 1995 8:40 p.m.

My dear, dear Isaac.
    To be or not to be-
        Are you there?
            Are you inside me?

They tell me, "yes"; they tell me, "no"; I say, "I don't care"; I just want to know one way or the other. I saw the OB doctor today. I'm not very happy with what he said, saw or did. But time will tell.

First he said I would miscarry you and that you are not healthy; you are too small to even claim existence. Then, well, somewhere he did an ultrasound and could find no black spot (carrier of liquid) except my bladder. He couldn't find a sac with you in it. Then he poked and said my womb had no one in it that he could tell.

Are you there, Isaac?
Are you OK?

Then he took my blood and said he wouldn't be able to tell me about the result until tomorrow.

Isaac, he said you would die, if you hadn't already.
I was so sad!

I came home and went to see Ruth and told her everything I could in an hour. She said, "Yes, go see Pastor," so I'm hoping Dad will go with me.

I came home for supper. Could you tell I ate spicy taco salad? Becky made it all and Josh grated the cheese, and I told your family what the doctor said. They kept talking about your name. They don't believe the doctor! Dad still thinks you're coming. But we remembered, Dad and I, that my doctor told me Becky wasn't coming until I saw him a month later, and then he told me I was two months pregnant!

I don't know if you are. And if you are, I don't know how you are! But I love you just the same. I am exhausted. Last night I slept, but I didn't get up for a snack or to use the bathroom. Are you still there? "[God] grants sleep to those he loves." (Psalm 127:2d NIV) I guess God knew I needed adequate rest to make it through a traumatic day. I pray He grants sleep again tonight.

Isaac, don't give up!
> We all love you.
>> We want to see you.

We're saving our hugs and kisses and snuggles and cuddles for you.
Well, maybe I'll give some to Dad! We'll share them with you for now.

Sleep and grow kid!

Love,
Mom

Tuesday, January 31, 1995

Isaac died.
> I don't know when.

My doctor told me the blood test was negative, that is, it currently reported less than 3 for a count of human tissue. There must be a count of 10 before it is positive.

I miscarried. I don't know when. The bleeding I had was little and it stopped. I have no abdominal discomfort due to any remains of life that existed-for what?-three weeks?

Tim said the blood test was positive in the emergency room. I don't remember when I was there and I don't care. It doesn't matter. Nothing does, except that I see Pastor tomorrow.

Wednesday, February 1, 1995 8:26 a.m.

Dear Isaac,

Are you with Jesus now? Did you give Grandma Punke a hug from me? By the grace of God, I will see you someday, Isaac, as God enables me.

The desire of my heart has always been and always will be to have babies. But I have another desire too: I desire to play organ for Jesus at church, and next time I play, I think, is February 26 and when I say thank you to Jesus this time, I will specifically thank Him for giving you to me and for taking you back again.

This is my last letter, Isaac. I'd rather deliver my hugs and kisses in person.

See you soon,
Mom

———————

Thursday, February 2, 1995 9:18 p.m.

My baby is dead.
    I am half dead.
        I am numb-there is no life in me.

I breathe because I have to. I eat and sleep and go to the bathroom because I have to.

———————

Friday, July 26, 1996

My dear Isaac,

I just wanted to tell you I went swimming at Camp Phillip today, and I thought about you swimming too.

It was interesting how it happened. Your big brother, Josh, was at Doug Collins basketball camp. After I came home from the Worship Conference in Kenosha on Wednesday, Dad and I went to pick up Josh at Concordia River Forest on Thursday. We spent the night at Grandpa Punke's in Brookfield, WI.

The next morning we went to get the dent fixed in Josh's trumpet before picking up Becky at camp. We drove to Camp Phillip, but she was at Camp Tiwaushara, which we had already passed. While Dad and Josh went to get directions, I hurried to go swimming. I wanted to go swimming at Camp Phillip because I knew I wouldn't be too sad if I remembered you there.

I didn't cry, Isaac. I just remembered how much I love you.

You know what? I gave Becky her piccolo on the way home from camp. It is her confirmation present. You know what else? Dad and another lady may sing "Another Child to Hold" at the Lutherans for Life banquet on September 20, just after your first birthday.

See you soon,
Mom

COMFORT

A Card From Faith

Thinking of you...

Oh, Luann! Warm thoughts and prayers are with you in your sorrow. (after I lost Isaac) If only I could wrap my arms around you and hold you. How faithful you have been to us! Praying, even bringing me water when we were in Crete.

God has your name written on His walls and baby's too. How comforting to know!

See, now we peer through darkened windows trying hard to see with understanding, but one day it will all be clear.

1 Thessalonians 5:10 (NIV) reads, "He died for us so that, whether we are awake or asleep, we may live together with him." Just think of the parties we will have in heaven; time and miles will no longer separate us. What a joyous time that will be!

Jude 24 (NIV) reads, "...he is able to keep you from falling and to present you before his glorious presence without fault and with great joy--to the only God..."

Place your whole self in God's comforting hands. Just lay all your hurt and sorrow and loneliness for Him to wash away. He can do it like no other. Snuggle up to God. He loves you more than any of us will ever realize. Through our trials we come to know Him better and our walk becomes stronger.

You know these things! Your prayer life and devotional life is strong. You and Ann W are tops on the prayer warrior list!!

Know, Luann, in our heart, that the thoughts of your dear friends reach out to you, and I carry love and comfort to you, even though we are miles away.

In the Lamb,

Hugs and kisses,
Faith

Baby Tears

We cried tears when we learned that a child would
be, that your GOD had allowed you to quicken in
me. We cried tears with our loved ones as they shared
our joy, and we thought about names for a girl or a
boy. I cried tears as I thought of the things that we
would do, all the things that your Daddy would pass
on to you. And I cried as I thought of each inch you
had grown, as I pondered the day you'd make yourself known. Then, to think of the world you must
enter brought tears. Once again, little loved one, your
Mother cried tears.

Something's wrong. I can tell--once again there are
tears, and I'll not get the chance of your love through
the years. Oh the ache and the sorrow and all of the
pain, and again, yes again, my tears fell like rain. Then
His peace comes to me as I think of you there, gently
rocking with FATHER in His favorite chair. Your
sweet little fingers clenched tight in His palm and
His SON softly singing to help keep you calm. Our
FATHER knew your days before they came to be,
and He knew, little one, you would not stay with me.

So, I cry but I know that when this life is done, I will
greet and embrace you my little sweet one. There's a
time to be born and a time to die, and the joy and the
sorrow both make us cry!

-Conni Johnson

Luann's Song (Joni's Waltz)

Though God gives me not another child to bear,
I refuse to live a life of deep despair
God may not grant this desire But with love my heart's inspired
For He has given me a gift beyond compare.

   *For heaven is dearer to me And at times it is all I can see
   And sweet music I hear Coming down to my ear
   And I know that it's playing for me.
   For I am Christ, the Savior's own bride
   And redeemed I shall stand by his side.
   He will say, "Shall we dance?"
   And our endless romance will be worth all the tears I have cried.

On that special day when our lives became one
We found our times of greatest joy had just begun
And in our role as man and wife God began a brand new life
Within the year I'd given birth to our first son. But still heaven…

When I had our little girl upon my breast
She was taken that I might get needed rest
For the while I was insane I have never known such pain
It was by far the Savior's very hardest test.

For He wanted me to know how filled with pride
Was my life both on the out and the inside
But instead of showing wrath He's shed His light upon my path
That forevermore with Him I may abide. That's why heaven…

*I rejoice with him whose pain my Savior heals
And I weep with him who still his anguish feels
But earthly joys and earthly tears Are confined to earthly years
And a greater good the Word of God reveals.

*In this life we have a cross that we must bear
A tiny part of Jesus' death that we can share
And one day we'll lay it down For he has promised us a crown
To which our suf-fer-ing can never be compared. That's why heaven...

Now later after ten long years of rest
We both seek our God to do what He sees best
May He show to us His will No matter what, we'll love Him still
And we'll serve him now with even greater zest. For heaven...

*Joni Eareckson Tada's verses

I wrote the verses for Luann's song about our family and used Joni's verses for the ones that were not specifically about our family. I wrote them for a ceremony to renew our vows - just the four of us (Tim and I, Josh and Becky). I made Tim a lemon meringue pie and used freshly squeezed lemons.

Somewhere In The World

Wayne Watson

Somewhere in the world today
A little girl will go out to play
All dressed up in Mama's clothes
At least the way that I suppose it goes
Somewhere in the world tonight
Before she reaches to turn out the light
She'll be prayin' from a tender heart
The simple prayer that's a work of art

And I don't even know her name
But I'm prayin' for her just the same
That the Lord will write His name upon her heart
'Cause somewhere in the course of this life
A little boy will need a godly wife
So, hold on to Jesus, baby, wherever you are.

Somewhere in the world out there
That little girl is learning how to care.
She's pickin' up her Mama's charms
Or maybe swingin' 'round in her Daddy's arms
Somewhere in the world to be
Though the future's not real clear to me
Theirs could be a tender love
Grounded in eternal love.

And I don't even know her name
But I'm prayin' for her just the same
That the Lord will write His name upon her heart
'Cause somewhere in the course of this life
My little boy will need a godly wife
So hold on to Jesus, baby, wherever you are.

Hold on to Jesus, baby, wherever you are.

DIVINE CALL FOR MY PASTOR

1991

Dear Luann,

Whether the times are good or bad, successful or difficult; whether God seems near or far, God is faithful and will not forsake his own. You have witnessed his faithfulness and you are a faithful witness of his grace that never fails. May God bless you in your continuing walk with him. He'll always be there. He is God--yours and ours in Christ.

In His Name,
H. Curtis Lyon

Philippians 4:7 (NIV). "And the peace of God, which transcends all understanding, will guard your hearts and your minds in Christ Jesus."

(This is what my pastor wrote to me in the book he authored: "Counseling At the Cross".)

April 1996

Forgive me if this letter is out of place. I want to share these thoughts with you and I don't know that I'll get to come and see you. Please bear with me.

"A neighbor living nearby is better than a brother far away." (Prov. 27:10c NET)

I was troubled to hear you had a Call. I will continue praying that God give you wisdom as you decide where to serve Him. Most of this year (1996) I have been praying selfishly for you to stay, if indeed you received a Call. That is why I said I will continue to pray for you.

Pastor, others can preach, others can teach, others can counsel---
truthfully, I don't feel I need you like I used to feel I did.
"Do not abandon your friend or your father's friend..." (Prov. 27:10 a NET)

I have made so many mistakes--a lot of them you know. They are painful reminders of my weakness and joyful reminders of God's grace. "Do not go to your brother's home when you are in trouble." (Prov. 27:10b NET) Part of me cries out, "LEAVE!"

BUT, I would be too sad if you go--

It is a privilege to work with you in church. I feel the "enemy" has tried very hard to destroy that working relationship. It is a victory celebration for me each time I can work with you.

I'm glad you could work with Becky this year for confirmation class. There's only one more year for her. I'd like you to be here.

Pastor, I don't know that I have the energy to search for, to get to know another friend like you. You and your family are dear to my heart. It may never rain in southern California, but if you leave, there will be tears falling in Crete.

June 1996

To Pastor Lyon, my pastor,

This is not a theological dissertation, it's just how I feel.

I think I have already told you before that I call you my pastor because you belong to me. Others claim the same possession and I'm willing to share. My father has six others who can call him "my father." And so I want you to remember that you are my pastor--not the most significant, not the most important, not the most influential, not the only pastor for me--just my pastor, because you belong to me. Though my father is the only father I'll ever have, there are others who have been and will be my pastor.

Though you are leaving to go to California, I want you to know you will still be my pastor because you belong to me. It seems to me that you belong to me, not because I bought you, but because you made an investment in my life. I greatly appreciate the time that you freely gave me as you made that investment. I pray that, though you or I may never fully realize the final result of that investment, that God will richly reward you for investing wisely.

It is interesting how God prepared my heart. I have shed so many tears--every time you've received a Call--just pretending you would leave. This time I got so sick of leaning one way and then the other, that I just quit leaning at all. About a week ago it was as if my prayers subconsciously changed from, "Help Pastor decide your will," to "Help me accept Pastor's decision." I "knew", I just had a "funny feeling" you would leave, but until you actually announced it, I could still hope you would stay… BUT now I can rest. Now I can work with this decision.

I will miss you sorely. I will miss your teasing. I will miss the music of your voice when you preach. I won't be able to go past your old house without praying for you and yours.

But, I am excited for the people in California and I am excited for what God will do here at Trinity.

Pastor, I think I've told you that the rain reminds me that God is in control. Perhaps God sent all this rain just to convince me that He can take care of things here at Trinity, that He can take care of me even when you go to California.

And so you told us you are going to California. It took me a whole service to realize Ann is going too! YIKES!!--a pastor we can replace, but Ann! It didn't really bother me to lose our 1st grade teacher because that won't affect me or my kids. Tim is not happy. But who will tell me when I play organ? Who will play for funerals and weddings?

Then I started to pray for God to grant an increase on the investment you've made in my life. Tim already asked me to play for the Senior choir. That's exciting!
I am happy and excited for you to go to California, but I am so sad to have you leave Crete. I am excited to see what mighty work God will do at Trinity in taking away two pastors in the course of one week.

Probably the hardest thing for me is to think that I will never hear from you or be able to talk to you after you go to California. And so I will let God be in control and handle that one. Other pastors have invested in my life, but you have had more opportunity than any of the others. Thank you for being my pastor.

What God ordains is always good   His will abideth holy.
As He directs my life for me   I follow meek and lowly.
My God indeed   In every need   Doth well know how to shield me.
To Him then I will yield me.

What God ordains is always good   He never will deceive me.
He leads me in His own right way   And never will He leave me.
I take content   What He hath sent   The hand that brings me sadness
Will turn my tears to gladness.

(The Lutheran Hymnal 521 verses 1 & 2)

Farewell Poem for Pastor Lyon

Dear Pastor Lyon's set to go
We're sad to see him part
You wouldn't leave unless, we know,
The Lord spoke to your heart.

We're thankful for the faithful years
You worked among us here
To know that won't hold back the tears
For one we hold so dear.

You've got so many years now past
The rest should be no chore
God's blessed you from the first to last
And has much more in store.

From Chicago where you first began
Through College, Prep and Sem
God lead your path from child to man
As He bestowed each gem.

You vicared and were thought so nice
In Alpine on the coast
The Lord chose you to do it twice
With Crete your second post.

Then off to Zion way out west
You trekked to your first Call
Till Trinity sent it's request
And God said, "Go!" (like Paul)

And through it all dear Ann was there
To share your bliss and tears
You thought no offspring was your share
Not seven in ten years!

Of talents, we must all confess
You showed more than good looks
Collecting thoughts on crisis stress
To fill two helpful books.

Your doctor's bag bag so black and deep
You take as needs arrive
Proclaims your great desire to keep
Bodies and souls alive.

Another skill you've used before
Is found in Joseph's trade
An altar, lectern, desk and more
With humble hands you've made.

Computer work is just one way
You serve the Lord high-tech
It follows quickly plans you lay
And almost never wreck.

You've brightened up our lives for years
You've shared our joys and tears
You've cared and cheered and helped before
You've done it all and more.

You've helped me regain my desire to live
You've helped us to see what we have to give
And whether we went to the depths or the heights
You always kept Jesus' cross in sight.

And so we offer thanks to you
With all God's blessings too
We're grateful for the way you've cared
And for the love you've shared.

DIVINE CALL FOR MY PASTOR

Pastor, thank you for the time you've spent
To help us in our need
We know you're surely "heaven-sent"
God's sheep and lambs to feed.

God's blessed you through the years that sped
Down paths not always planned
And though unsure what lies ahead
You know you're in His hand.

Our pastor, counselor, brother and friend
Has found it's time to depart
God's Spirit send this void to mend
And to restore joy to our hearts.

Len Punke

I sent the information about Pastor Lyon to Len and he put it in the poem above.

Sunday, August 11 6:45 p.m.

Today was Pastor Lyon's last service at Trinity. Today was his farewell dinner.

Church went well. I played the organ. Daddy came to pick up Lowell and stayed to go to church and for the farewell.

Mindy, Kelly and Becky played flute-Oh that the Lord Would Guide My Ways, I Am Jesus' Little Lamb-offertory (Becky), O Jesus Grant Us Hope and Comfort and Trumpet Voluntary with three flutes.

Pastor picked some great hymns:
(can't remember the first one)-four flats-a new hymn-singable

Oh That the Lord Would Guide My Ways, The Alleluia Hymn
and the closing hymn - How Great Thou Art

The farewell went fine. We couldn't do Jesus Name Above All Names
because we couldn't copy it. That was ok. I said, "Pastor, whether times
are good or bad, whether we're happy or sad, you would have us glory
in the cross of Christ." Then we sang "In the Cross of Christ I Glory"
(Josh on piano, me on guitar) Then I read Len's poem. Doug put it in
a frame for Pastor. We ended with "Go My Children" with guitar.

Then we put everything away--just waiting to go through the line to
say goodbye to the Lyons.

Finally I decided I couldn't wait any longer; I had to get it over!

I just looked at my Pastor and he looked at me. Then I gave him a hug
and said I didn't want to go to church because I couldn't shake his hand.
He never said anything to me. As I quit hugging him, I grabbed his
hands and said, "I'll miss you." Then I turned away to cry.

Ann gave me a hug and said the music went well and that I don't need
them anymore because I'm strong. I told her I would still be sad.

Becky said that Pastor told her to keep running and he told Josh he'd
probably dunk this year.

He told Tim to call any time and wished him God's blessings in Crete.

He said nothing to me--that almost means more than if he'd said some-
thing-he didn't know what to say?

———————

Tuesday, August 14, 1996 12:06 a.m. midnight

My father is 73 today.

Lyons left today--not until 6:30 p.m.

I saw the moving truck when I went to Bible class at 9:30. I wanted to hurry home so I wouldn't miss the moving truck leaving.

I watched all day from my porch.

I took a picture of the truck at their house before I left for Bible class. Then it turned the corner and went to school--about 4:00--and I took a picture of the truck at Trinity (at church) Phyllis was here now. She sat with me on my porch until 6:30 when they drove away in two cars I took a picture when the truck came back to their house and when both cars drove away.

I had a hollow feeling in my stomach all day and I still do.

CORRESPONDENCE

1/20/99 6:30 p.m. Wed

Dear Ann and all,

I met one of your friends today. He was thrilled to get your Christmas letter and said at least three times what nice people you are. He said he has a lot of customers because of you. Did you guess?

I met your eye doctor today. It happened this way:

This actually started this weekend when I spent an hour shoveling the stepped-on ice off our sidewalk and asked Tim to finish getting the slush off the driveway while it was still melting, before dark. Tim refused to be told what to do, so I yelled and screamed. Brent and David were outside getting back from the flower shop, as it was the night of the Homecoming dance. I'm sure they heard me yell and scream!

Sunday I didn't want to take communion since Tim was assisting, but Joyce called and told me she was going to play for me while I went up to the Lord's table. So I had no choice, but I didn't know that I should be there. When I apologized to Tim for yelling, he apologized IF he offended me. Things seemed worse instead of better.

Monday we had Civil Rights Day off, and Tuesday I walked to school for my lessons. I slipped at the end of the driveway, as freshly fallen snow had covered the ice. I ended up flat on my back and thought twice about getting right back up. After work I taught two piano lessons and decided to shovel. It only made sense as I was home and had nothing else to do. I shoveled a path for the mailman and shoveled up the steps of our porch by the mailbox. I slipped as I turned to go back down the steps and quickly shifted my weight to remain upright, only to jab my right eye with the handle of the shovel.

I called Tim, and he said he would try to come in a half hour, but he didn't. I called Rose, and she said to call the pharmacist. He started talking about a detached retina and I got scared. I called Lynn; she was home, and she said I could go blind and to go see somebody. I'd already worried, called these people and had ice on my eye for 20 minutes, and still no Tim! So I called Pam, and she sent Joe right over and said they would get Tim. Joe said I looked OK and told Tim, who came, that I had talked to too many people that were making me worried. Joe said to call the eye doctor. He was out of the office and had no hours on Wednesday, but he came just to see me! I had scratched my cornea and he told me I would be better in 48 hours or something small like that. He didn't do a six hour dilation test, but told me I would know if there was anything more that was wrong.

He was very nice and was very glad to hear that I had seen you and could tell him about your wonderful house.
I know yelling and screaming at Tim was not good judgement on my part, but don't you think God could have come up with something other than a black eye and a scratched cornea to get Tim to shovel?

Regarding the 150th anniversary at Trinity

The first chance I had after I got back from California, I talked to Doug about why you had heard nothing about the anniversary. He sent me to Bill. I actually reached him by phone. He explained that since you are so far away, "they" didn't want to pay travel expenses. He also said that you hadn't been gone very long, and "they" wondered if it was wise to have you come. So I said, not speaking for you, that telling you nothing about the 150th anniversary celebration was not good. I also said there may be times when you would be in the area and could possibly make Crete a stop. Bill said he would write to you. I hope you've heard something by now!

We saw a marriage counselor on January 7th. He said I have SAD eyes and that Tim cannot make up for all the sadness in my past, but that we can work on it now. He asked what homework we would give ourselves. (A lady was there too.) Tim said to hug more. I didn't know what to say, so I said to read the Bible and pray together. Then the counselor asked if I could add to that. I already felt that what I'd said was impossible. He asked me to pick one thing I need and give Tim a multiple choice of how or when to meet that need. So I asked, "HOW DO I GET TIM'S ATTENTION?" and the counselor said, "WHATEVER IT TAKES!" I was SAD because that seemed way too hard.

Pastor, I was also sad because Tim said he had talked to you twice last year, not because you talked, but because Tim didn't tell me.

Friday, January 22

We met with our counselors last night. We were told that we give each other messages (Tim to Luann-"You're really not important." Luann to Tim-"You never do enough.") He said listening to us talk about our schedule is exhausting. Tim does not sense anything is missing in our relationship. I was asked to define what is missing by our next session.

Basketball news: Josh has only eight on his team (at Joliet) now, due to quitting or grades. He said it is harder to get in the game now than it was with thirteen on the team. Coach plays six men and Josh and his second roommate watch. Josh isn't really sure he even wants to get in now; he's had no experience in a real game. Josh will be a better coach knowing how it is to be the Big Man on the team and a bench warmer. He told us he may go to MLC next year. His buddy, Tim, is thinking about it too. He told Josh they should go now as nothing may transfer.

Becky has been seeing a lot of playing time. She scored 29 at Mooseheart, 22 at Westminster, 25 at Christ Lutheran, 11 at LaLumiere (Heidi was high point with 16!), and last night 23 at Luther East with instructions to NOT SHOOT! She would have made the 30 points Dad said he would give her $10 for!! She's had a lot of assists too.

Know anything about fuel injection? Josh's car died at Joliet, and there was gas all over, even in the air filter. Midas fixed it for over $500. (So much for being ahead with saving to pay our taxes.)

I will remember our trip to California for a long time. It was perfect from top to bottom! I thank God I had a chance to come and see you. Palm Springs was really nice, but I bought two plane tickets to come and see you!!

Bye for now,
Luann

———————————

July 9, 1999

I'm going to try to write several letters at once. My plan is to write general info to all of you, copy my letter, and then include personal messages.

We will install our new pastor this Sunday! I'm the organist, and Tim will probably play the trumpet. Our new pastor plays violin, tuba, and trombone!! Our senior pastor wondered if he'd get help in the pulpit! It will be nice to have two pastors again. I hope we can start an evening midweek Bible class.

Tim and I were seeing a counselor but we plan to discontinue those visits due to a mess-up with filing the insurance claim. I asked in the beginning that he file under Tim's name, but he forgot to tell his secretary. Our former counselor always filed under Tim's name, so I know it can be done. But now that filing is messed up, we were told that it cannot be corrected. So, Tim is planning to call and cancel when he is home today.

Tim just spent three weeks at the Sem and has completed all the credits needed for a Master's degree in historical theology. What a blessing! He must take a three hour test before he graduates.

Our neighbors moved to Wisconsin and left a lot of stuff in their house. The house was not fit to be inhabited so our senior pastor is moving to the farm estate to make room in the house they were in for our new teacher and part of their seven children. I say part, because one of them is in college. I can hardly wait till they come! The husband was a year ahead of Tim at DMLC and I know his wife a little too.

The Rimpel's have a pool! Josh can lay down in it. I use it more than anyone else. Basically, I just get wet and walk around in my wet swimsuit to stay cool. The rust settles after a week or so, and then we have to scrub it out and change the water. That's a hassle!

Becky is at a youth rally in Ottawa, Canada. She's on the 17th floor of a Radisson Hotel-wonderful! I am so thankful for Wittes and Laubers being chaperones.

Josh works long hours at a factory for personal products. He's at least a half hour away and works twelve hour shifts: on two days, off two or three days. He plans to visit his grandma and grandpa later this month on his days off. He is bringing in two to three hundred a week. That helps!!

Sunday, August 22, 1999

Dear Loriena,

You asked about my diet, so I decided to write this down for my own sake and to share my struggle with you as well.

I was never on a diet as a child, teen or young mother. "Spy it, try it!", was my motto. I was troubled to hear Tim's mom tell me there would come a time when I would no longer be able to eat anything I wanted, and she assured me I would get fat. Since that time I have been conscious of my weight; it has almost become an obsession and I don't like that!

My first attempt at a diet was due to a very annoying wart on my pointer finger tip. A friend suggested separating grains. It was a four day rotation: corn or wheat/ oats/ rice/ rye. I could eat any meat, fruit or vegetable, but I tried really hard to eat only the grain of the day. That was hard while feeding my family too. The result: the wart that had been cauterized once and frozen off twice was gone!! And, my immune system was strengthened.

I went for a checkup to a doctor in Indiana and was put on a very strict diet for hypoglycemia. This was a low carbohydrate diet. I tried it for a while and found I was losing weight (my rings were loose) and I was always hungry. In my life-style, I can't be eating a main course meal while "on the run", in between things. I'm lucky to get a main course meal at supper. I was frustrated and gave up, except for eating lots of vegetables. I returned to my normal weight. I began to allow sweets again and now I tip the scale about five pounds over what I'd like to weigh. And I am paranoid, because five can become ten and so on…

This past spring I went to a ladie's retreat in Wisconsin and ate lunch with a friend of my sister. This lady had also read the book, "Fit For Life," by the Diamonds. I had read it, but didn't really think it would work. They advocated just fruit in the morning, salad or cucumber, avocado or tomato sandwiches for lunch and meat and vegetables for supper. Having spoken with someone who really said this worked, I borrowed the book from the library and got some recipes. I tried some of them this summer while Tim was at the seminary. I don't like rice, spinach and zucchini mixed together. I liked this book and the recipes because they explained that your body needs one kind of digestive juice, alkaline (?), to digest meat and the other, acid, to digest carbohydrates. Therefore, according to them, you just don't eat meat with potatoes, rice or pasta.

BUT I ALWAYS EAT MEAT WITH POTATOES, RICE OR PASTA!!

I don't like to eat meat alone. I don't like to be hungry all the time. I need to eat things that will stay with me and fuel my active life-style.

You seemed to have a diet that really worked for you. That is why I persisted in asking you what you eat. If it works, really works for you, maybe it would work for me. I don't even have time to think about cooking differently. It is a major chore to put a meal on the table at all.

Better go---
Luann

Afghans

On Friday, June 18, I saw Mandy, Rachel and Wendy. They told me Kristin was getting married in August and that her bridesmaid dresses would be lavender. I decided I would try to make Don and Kistin an afghan, even though I have three to make for next spring. I wanted to try. In the process I ran into a few roadblocks.

We took Tim out for Father's Day, because we found a wallet with a $20 bill that no one claimed. Since we were close, I asked if we could stop at Walmart, the only store I know that still carries yarn. Becky helped me pick the yarn. The color label said, "light amethyst." It was Red Heart Soft yarn. I didn't realize it was going to work up so differently.

Anyway, I was glad Josh came in because I had no means to pay-no cash, no card! I figured we could just use Josh's. Josh did not have pockets and did not have his card. He went to get his dad. Tim sent back his wallet and I thought, "Maybe they won't check." But they check the signature at Walmart. Tim had not even signed his card! Josh went to get Dad. Tim charged the yarn. (That is Tim's contribution.)

So, I could start. I worked all day on Sunday and had the start of a nice baby afghan! Yikes! The smaller yarn worked up just beautifully, but it was too small. I started over with more stitches. I had to finish a skein of yarn to know how far a skein would go, and then I could estimate how many skeins I would need. I had stripped the Matteson Walmart of all the Red Heart Soft light amethyst yarn. I determined Tuesday that I would need at least three more skeins.

The Matteson Walmart said they would get no more of this yarn and suggested I try another store. I called Orland Park, and they had some. They held it until Josh took me to pick it up on Wednesday. I did about six rows while Josh drove. (That is Josh's contribution.)

Becky said, "Wow! You're getting pretty far," "that's pretty," and other encouraging remarks. (That is Becky's contribution.)

Your afghan almost covers my lap. From here it is one stitch at a time.

PS When my oldest nephew reached confirmation upon completion of 8th grade, I decided to make an afghan for each of my nieces and nephews for confirmation gifts. God blessed, and I did succeed in making 32 afghans! I haven't made one for Jacob yet. When Pastor's kids got married, I tried to make one for them too.

> With every stitch I've said a prayer
> That God would keep you in His care.
> I've said this prayer so many times
> I've counted to 9,999
> So God will surely answer this
> He'll take you to eternal bliss.
> "She makes coverings for her bed..."
> (Proverbs 31:22a NIV)

January 23, 2000

I was concerned when Becky showed me your name in the bulletin. Then I saw your mom at Bible class and was able to ask why.

"Praise be to the God and Father of our Lord Jesus Christ, the Father of compassion and the God of all comfort, who comforts us in all our troubles, so that we can comfort those in any trouble with the comfort we ourselves have received from God." (2 Corinthians 1:3-4)

I am so very sad with you. I praise God he spared your life. When I heard about your pregnancy and surgery, I had a hard time making it through Bible class. I'm enclosing two things.

In 1995, just after two single girls gave birth, I got pregnant. Our son would be-what, 5 years old this September. When I found out I was pregnant, I named our child "Isaac" for it was indeed cause to LAUGH! By the time I saw a doctor, I was spotting and no longer pregnant. The loss of my baby was very hard for me, but Tim had a hard time relating. He handled the loss rather quickly. But for me it was different. I named our baby "Isaac" and I offered him to God, just like Abraham. But, unlike Abraham, God did take my "son." Shortly after this I found the poem "Baby Tears" and that is the first enclosure. When I think of our baby in heaven with Jesus--here's the chorus of a song:

> Heaven is dearer to me And at times it is all I can see
> And sweet music I hear coming down to my ear
> And I know that it's playing for me.
> For I am Christ the Savior's own Bride
> And redeemed I shall stand by His side
> He will say, "Shall we dance?" and our endless romance
> Will be worth all the tears I have cried.
>
> Joni Eareckson Tada

The poem Baby Tears is hung beside my bed by a picture of me holding Josh when he was about a month old. And I remember my great loss.

Months after my miscarriage, I was awake at 4:00 a.m. and listening to WMBI with Mike Kellog (90.1 FM). He played "Another Child to Hold" by Ray Boltz. I was able to understand better the concept of giving my child to Jesus.

It was very hard for me to understand God's ways--why he allowed two babies to unwed mothers and why He took mine. Surely, He knew I would have loved my baby! It didn't pay to wonder for long. I

needed someplace to go and Jesus was available. "Each heart knows its own bitterness and no one else can share its joy." (Proverbs 14:10 NIV) I knew only Jesus could really understand my sorrow. I knew He cared about me and how I felt about it all, and I knew He would help me through it.
You are in my prayers.

With love,
Luann Rimpel

1 Peter 3:15 "Always be ready.." (personal paraphrase)

January 8, 2001
9:00 a.m.

Dear Pastor,

I'm thinking of Proverbs 20:5 where the NIV reads, "The purposes of a man's heart are deep waters, but a man of understanding draws them out." Your name is in my Bible by that verse, and it is circled in red. I'm back to carrying my NIV (my wedding gift from Tim) because Tim didn't like God's Word to the Nations.

So, what is the purpose of this letter? I wondered if you would just LISTEN, ok? This letter is addressed to you, but if it is sharable, I don't care if you share it. If you'd like to burn it, that's ok too. I talk mostly to Ann, and so I write mostly to you.

Thank you for the multiple invitations to stay at your house, but as long as Tim is in Crete, I'm more comfortable staying in Palm Springs. You have to be nuts to drive 2000 miles over mountains and through the desert, for what? The ocean was fine, the parade was fine, actually they were wonderful! But, I drove 2000 miles to come and see you! I hope that makes you feel special.

Your mom is doing incredibly well! How sweet of her to come out-side to tell me 'who was who" in Rachel's wedding pictures. She said I must be pretty special, because you gave me three oranges, the oranges you waited so long to get! I told her you are special too. If I didn't say much about how sweet and juicy and yummy the orange I ate was, it was because I was so happy to have them. I did share the other two with Josh, Becky and Aaron, but mostly I ate them myself.

We told you a bit about our car trip to California. The engine coolant light went on BEFORE we saw the mountains, but Jack said he'd take care of it in Palm Springs! Listen to this: No sooner did we lose Jack and the other retired couple, (we waited for Josh and Aaron to catch up to us so we were together), than the needle went straight to HOT! You know a lot about cars. It was never warm, just hot when we were separated. We were in Avon, a town with many round-a-bouts. The four of us got off on the wrong corner of the circle, and that's when the temperature said hot. Josh and Aaron had to go get coolant and water, which was a feat in itself in that screwy town. We used the front of my notebook to make a funnel to pour it in. I don't remember exactly how it worked out. We went to a gas station, but we were sent to a Lincoln dealership, just down the road. Imagine that! Before we ever got to the gas station, we added still more coolant and water and started the car with the cap off, and it appeared that everything we poured in bubbled over and out!

Now, how do you think I was by this time?

I was ok! I know why I like to travel. It helps me keep my priorities in line. God was going to have to get us through this. We had the town, the name of the motel and the 800 number for the motel where we were to spend the night. We hoped to meet up with Jack there.

When we started our trip, Becky had the stomach flu, Josh wasn't feeling well and I knew I'd be feeling lousy soon. Becky drove a little that first day. I drove twice, and then Josh and Aaron drove. Becky drove a lot the second day. The third day, I drove through the desert and then, we were in California. We had three days: we saw the ocean, came to church, and saw the Rose Bowl Parade. The most sun I got was sitting in your backyard. I wish we'd had more time to sunbathe and swim. But it was still a great trip until we came home.

Tim picked us up at Midway. He couldn't find a place to park, so he risked getting a $100 fine from parking in the handicapped parking. Our flights were great. The second flight waited for the Chicago people! So, at Midway, we were waiting and waiting for our luggage, and looking for Tim. Once we had our luggage, all of it, I stayed with the luggage and the other three went looking for Tim. They found him in two minutes. He didn't seem very happy to see me, but that was because he wanted to get out of that parking spot. But, he seemed happier to see Becky. I was so happy to see him! We got in the van and had NO HEAT, NO DEFROST, NO BLOWER, and it was about 5 degrees. Welcome back!! It was good to be home.

Once home and warm, I could collect my thoughts. I was feeling somewhat miserable, and I realized I was once again dealing with an emotional toll factor. Everything about our trip was wonderful, but the news about Rachel's baby was not wonderful. I don't remember how I responded when I was told she was pregnant and due in May, but I do remember how I felt. I felt sick, sick to my stomach. I usually feel pretty bad when I feel sick.

Then, my heart felt very heavy. I needed Tim to hold me; I've also needed klonopin for five nights out of the last seven. Klonopin is what I take to help me go to sleep when the 7.5 mg of zyprexa isn't doing it.

I need to proceed with caution. I'll have to relax earlier and drink extra chamomile tea and, well. I could work on Rachel's afghan. It is started now. Starting is the hardest part. Crocheting the rest is just tedious. I'm just afraid I won't have time to finish it. I'll probably send it to you. My plan is to get it done this winter.

Guess what? I'm playing for a wedding on January 13th. Guess what? Women's Gathering is meeting for Prayer, Praise, Exercise and Laughter. I plan to lead a devotion on prayer, play some praise songs to sing along with, lead some aerobic exercises from a record I used with Josh and Becky (just the warmup and cooldown) and a couple from a record of aerobics to Christian music, and then we will play Carrom, a game with circle pieces you "ping" across a board the size of a card table. The object is to get your color in the corner pockets and hinder your opponent from doing the same. That should be good for a few laughs!

And so, I have to get it all together!! The spotlight is not always a very good place for me to be, so one of my friends is helping me.

I retyped "Isaac's Diary", the diary of the baby I lost in 1995. I've also sorted through all my old diaries and torn out pages to keep. Now I want to burn the rest of the pages, but I don't know where to build a fire.

Did you hear that the current plan for our fellowship hall would remove all three houses on the church block? May God provide!

I know Rachel is not my daughter. I shouldn't be so upset. But she's your daughter. And so I am sad. And I am also well aware of the fact that I am no better than she is. May God have mercy!

Christ the Vine Evangelical Lutheran Church

July 6, 2001

Dear Luann,

Thanks so much for your trouble. I appreciate very much that you were able to find this. (He asked me to send him his collection of the four Gospels sorted by similar accounts.) I have copied it and I appreciate all the notes that have come along with it. I can't figure out how the thing got lost, but then, I've lost things before. (Pastor called me when I was packing to move and I had just packed it up! It was in a box labeled "study." I found it, in answer to prayer.)

I was very sorry to hear about Marilyn. She was such a joy to have around. She will be missed by many people.

Thank you too for the kind gift you sent. I have been amazed and surprised that people have thought about this anniversary. I just kind of woke up one day and realized that last week I was ordained in Torrance, California and this week I have been in the ministry for 30 years. It seems like a long time when you think about it that way, but from my point of view the time seems very short. I will never forget the two-thirds of it that were spent in Crete.

Thanks again for your trouble.

Yours in Christ,
Curt

H. Curtis Lyon

———————

May 2002

Dear friends,

I have so much to say, but I will try to keep it short as you are very busy people too.

I saw my pastor Monday and told him about my friends at the Support Group. One almost succeeded in an attempt at suicide this time and another, who has had lots of tragedy in life, has not been open to the Scriptures. I was so discouraged because I had shared Bible verses with the first friend every day for the last few months and then there was a suicide attempt anyway. I felt a great loss. I hadn't even been able to give my friend a hug at the last meeting.

Sometimes Tim has missed his meetings to take me to the Support Group.

I shared my Ascension bulletin with the second friend: the troubles of this life are not worth comparing with the glory that will be revealed, in my Father's house are many mansions…, and the hymn, "Heaven is My Home." I highlighted those parts. The service was all written out and there was no indication that they were Bible verses, so I sent it off with a prayer that it would be read without knowing it was from the Bible.

I thought that Pastor would commend me for sharing the Gospel. Instead he asked me for what purpose I went to the Support Group. It appeared to him that I was giving more support than I was getting. Perhaps that was not the best thing for me.

I was very sad my friend tried to commit suicide. I am very sad at the thought of not seeing my friends at the Support Group. I agree with Pastor that I'm not really getting support, but where else can I go?

I called Natalie and she suggested talking to Tim. I told her how he comes home for supper and asks to eat in front of TV watching the news. Twice I've said, "I'd rather eat with you," so he eats and goes to watch TV, barely saying anything. She suggested that I try to talk to Tim when we are on the road to New Ulm Friday and back on Saturday. There would be no TV interference and there isn't usually very much on the radio worth listening to. I could tell him my concern about not getting support and ask if he could fill the gap. I could also ask him about the book I gave him at Christmas that has sat on a pile forgotten, "The Power of a Praying Husband" by Stormie Omartian. I'm not sure how to ask about that one.

Anyway, my reason for writing to you is because Natalie suggested you as people that could offer me support. On the computer I wouldn't be bothering you at a bad time. You can read and answer at your convenience.

Right now I am dealing with the loss of a friend to write to, the loss of my Support Group friends, and, in general, the lack of support from Tim. AND MY MUSIC RECITAL is Sunday at 2:00 at Zion. The losses are an emotional toll. That means I must proceed with caution.
As always, your prayers are appreciated. Know that you are in my prayers too.

God bless you,
Luann

Letters of Support

Dear Luann,

I just read your email. I tried to call you, but you're out and about. Thank you so much for sharing your heartfelt thoughts and feelings.

Your friends at the Support Group were fortunate to have you as their friend. You tried to guide them to the "one thing needful." I can understand Pastor's concern over your own personal edification, but I still think your friends were blessed to have your input as you shared your faith. One thing we needed always to remember in our own mission outreach was not to take rejection personally. It is the work of the Holy Spirit. If we personalize people's rejection then the danger is that we will take credit for those who come to faith in our Lord. But it is, never-the-less, troubling.

I will keep them and you in my prayers. Time is short right now, but I would like to have time with you to talk about these things. Perhaps we can arrange an afternoon tea, or morning get-together. I feel so privileged to be your personal friend.

In Christ's love,
Connie

"Ask and it will be given to you; seek and you will find; knock and the door will be opened to you." (Matthew 7:7 NIV)

I will pray for you. Having good friends is a real support and you should know that you do have a lot of friends that are with you. Those other people in that group can only help themselves now, and hopefully God will come into their hearts and they will find their Savior or that our Savior will find them and they will find the peace in their hearts that they need and that everyone needs. That is what has kept me going: knowing that God is with me and forgives me and just knowing that helps to put the peace in my heart. I need to be strong and go on.

I love living life and you are a very wonderful person who God has granted the talent of music to fill your heart and soul. Just trust in God and he will see you and all your needs and he will make your recital a most joyful sound to fill your heart with the peace that you need. And by giving yourself of your talent of music, you give joy to everyone that hears what you play or what someone has learned from you. You do have a lot to give and are always giving to others. You are a very compassionate person, but sometimes you do have to give to yourself as well and pray to God to give you the strength you need. You need to ask God to find your friends so he can find his way into their hearts.

Sometimes the things we try to do for others cannot be done as people do not always want to listen, but if God goes into their hearts, there will be no ignoring him. So just pray for them and take care of yourself. God is with you and so are your friends, if you need us. Do all these things and God will give you the peace you need in your heart.

Take care and remember that God loves you and so do I.

Your friend,
Sue

———————

Dear Luann,

I understand your being alone on this one. I have to say that the Lord brought me to a place in my life, where no one person, even if they were willing, could provide what I desperately needed. I was so dry spiritually. I prayed and prayed for spiritual healing and restoration of a joyful heart. He gave it to me. I now live with chronic vertigo, or the threat of impending vertigo. This means I would be flat in bed rendered helpless for several days to weeks. We have prayed for physical healing, as I have two young children to raise. But the greatest spiritual healing has occurred. I had to learn humility, because I had to depend on others. I learned dependence on the Lord for minute by minute needs. It has been a long journey, but I know it was needed.

May I suggest, without truly knowing your personal journey and struggles in life, that the Lord may want you to come to him first, and perhaps only, for your support? I do not intend this as any judgment or anything, but only that He seems to require this of us, especially at certain times in our walk. Perhaps you are at a point, healthy enough, that He may want you to lean on Him now and not so heavily on others, whether they be church or counseling relationships. I know you are such a witness for the Lord, and a faithful servant too!! I have seen your concern for others, your faith in action!!

My mother has gone through such a life! She was orphaned as a baby. At 17 she had to go into the world and make her way. She married my father, then he left her after 28 years. She always put herself so entirely into her relationships. One after another of her precious friends have died (cancer) or treated her so badly that they hurt her terribly. I have noticed a pattern of real dependence on these people. I have often said to her, that perhaps the Lord is asking her to rely on Him first, rather than on these others.

I understand your hurt and frustration with your unmet needs by your husband. We can only submit them to prayer, and genuinely ask the Lord to work in us first and foremost. As your friend, I will raise you up in prayer to the Lord. I am limited with my own challenges, but I appreciate you asking for support. Please realize that we are only here for such a short time, compared to eternity. Do not do anything to harm yourself. The race is almost over. Look up, and away from yourself, as you do, and minister to others. What a special gift you have been given to do so. May I suggest some good reading from the mystics, like Theresa of Avila, or perhaps Mother Theresa, any of the biographies of the saints who have given their entire lives solely to the Lord and his work. The one common thread is the lack of self-pity. I think we need to continually be grateful for all we do have, and look less at what we perceive we do not have.

With much love, and concern for you.
Salome

July 31, 2002
9:20 a.m.

Dear Pastor, my pastor,

I don't think I'll mail this letter right away. I don't care if anyone else reads this letter, but I'm going to pretend I'm talking to you, OK? I hope it's OK.

I went to talk to our pastor at Trinity. He said he could be Tim's brother. I thought, "Oh, great!" But that made me think of you, my other brother. I told Pastor I wanted to talk to Tim and asked if he could be there too. But, and Tim almost didn't tell me this, Pastor wanted to see only me. We talked for about an hour and a half. I kept waiting to go see Tim, or call him into the office, but I began to realize that I'd have no help talking to Tim.

I didn't feel very good, because I still had to talk to Tim. I did that as soon as we got home. I told Tim his careless comment about getting reimbursed for the Worship Conference had the same effect as if he had slugged me in the stomach. He apologized, and I accepted his apology. And I thought, "That's it?!"

I tried to talk to Tim earlier. We were in bed, and I told him I needed to talk to him. He said the next day at noon would work for him. Pastor said I should have talked to him right then and told him how his comment affected me. The next day at noon, he was so anxious to get back to school, I never brought it up. I was going to, but he was gone before I had a chance.

I feel like there was a tornado around me, but I was safe. Doesn't a tornado have a center point that is safe? The tornado around me was the "flu-like" symptoms and my frantic emails to my friends. (I didn't email you--that's good, huh?)

I think what happened to me was like an episode, but I was "awake" through it all. I never split from reality. What do you think? Why does this happen to me? I did so well at the whole Worship Conference, and then I came home.

I'd like to call, but I don't want to be a pest. I've bothered you enough. I'm thinking I might call in September, maybe.

PS I don't cry anymore. I am just numb.

I've been trying to watch what I eat for a year, but I can't lose the extra ten pounds. But with my "flu", I lost five pounds! But I still have five more to lose. I joined "Curves for Women," an exercise program a friend told me about at the Worship Conference. You only go three times a week for thirty minutes, but I still shouldn't eat like a pig!

———————

Monday, August 5, 2002
8:41

My job is going to be to fall in love with Tim again. "I can't help falling in love with you." (Elvis)

Is it true that Tim's comment really was NO BIG DEAL?

God bless you,
Luann

COURTSHIP

Sunday, February 17, 2002
6 p.m.

Dear Josh and Becky,

I thought you two might enjoy hearing about how Dad and I met and eventually married. Some of this you may know, but I thought it would be fun to tell you the story. Now, this is my perspective.

Dad had dated a few girls and nothing had worked out yet, so he was looking to try again. I had gone out with Dave and broken that off because I liked someone else who wasn't interested in me--a fellow oboe player. So, the guys at "The BIG E's" (Elsie Muetzel's basement) suggested that Uncle Len's sisters might be a good catch. Dad decided to ask the first one he saw. So, he asked Aunt Lana, and they went on a date. But Aunt Lana told Dad that she was dating someone back home and so, I think Dad asked her if I was available. My sister told me this guy might ask me out and encouraged me to go. I think what happened next was we passed each other down at St. Paul's at a youth meeting. I think that's when we decided to meet at the Music Center. This was in 1978, Dad's senior year.

Dad decided that we should try some of the songs he composed and that I could play my guitar. Well, Dad's songs were in a bunch of flats, not conducive to playing easy chords on guitar. Dad and I were in College Choir together. I figured out how to change the pitch of my guitar with a capo so I could play with Dad.

We never did anything fancy. I don't think we ever went to a movie. We walked around Flandrau Park a lot. We sat in Dad's car and talked.

We went to the Round Table for ice cream or downtown for pizza. We walked to church together.

Anyway, Dad went to Texas, I think, on a choir tour. While he was gone, I went back home and I made a patch-two connected hearts with our names embroidered on them. I thought this was all a dream. I remember making my bed with my dad and telling him I might marry Dad.

On the choir tour, Dad sang in Watertown and my family came to meet him. Back at school, we exchanged class rings. I told Dad I would wear his ring if I could sew my heart patch on my jacket.

We don't remember the exact date, but about seven weeks, seven being a number of completion or perfection, after we started dating we decided we would get married. BUT we decided not to tell anyone yet. We were going to wait until we went back home.

I don't remember how much time elapsed until the weekend we were gone on choir tour when Dad's roommate told the whole table of his friends that we were engaged. We had agreed to tell our roommates. Dad met me by the mailboxes and told me he had to talk to me. I thought he was going to break up with me. He said, "Dean let the cat out of the bag!" I didn't understand his expression, so he explained that his roommate had told a whole table of guys. By this time, everyone knew. I passed my good friend and she was really hurt that I hadn't told her. I said, "I didn't tell anyone!"

By this time we had planned how we would spend our summer. I returned to my room and my noteboard said to return a call to Massachusetts. I had signed up to be a nanny and had received a call to work with David, who had cerebral palsy. I did spend that summer in the Boston area with another friend. When Dad called, I cried, because he didn't sound the same. It was a long summer and I missed Dad a lot.

I still miss Dad a lot.

We didn't see each other very much my senior year because Dad was teaching here. He taught 6th grade and he had intermediate band and junior choir. It was a snowy winter. We got married the week after Uncle Len and I graduated from DMLC. That was hard on my mother. Some of my friends stayed at our house!!

We forgot to invite the parents of one of Tim's good friends. They stopped at Grandpa's house and offered us the use of their cabin on the lake to use for our honeymoon. We had planned to camp with Grandpa's trailer. I thought we would be gone for two weeks. Dad forgot to tell me he had volunteered me to teach Vacation Bible School the week after our wedding! I didn't talk to him all the way to the cabin. I didn't know how I could ever be ready to teach VBS. We got back to our apartment and I just bawled.

If I hadn't had the experience teaching VBS, it would have been harder to teach 1st grade. The Lord was my Help!

I forgot that I insisted that Dad call my dad and tell him of our plans to marry so he didn't hear it "through the grapevine." We called from the payphone by the mailboxes. Dad's knees were shaking.

We were going to wait two years to have kids, but that was not God's plan. I distinctly remember Dad's look of horror when I told him I thought I was pregnant. You see, it wasn't possible!!

The next hardest thing was having to leave Josh with a sitter when I taught Kindergarten at Zion. I cried all the way to school that first day. (I was walking.) I didn't want to teach another year so we planned Becky. I went to the doctor and was told I was not pregnant so I agreed to teach another year. The next time I went to the doctor, I found out that Becky was on the way!! So, both years I taught school, I was pregnant and sick to my stomach a lot. I had good classes and I loved teaching. I did not teach Kindergarten another year because Becky was born in November.

Once my sitter had sick kids so I had to find another mom to watch you. While you were there, Josh, you kept humming, "I Am Jesus' Little

Lamb." She asked if I sang that to you; she recognized the tune! You definitely sang before you talked very much.

So Becky came, but I was able to finish my year of teaching; it was half-day Kindergarten. I don't know if you remember what happened after that. It was October 1983 and I ended up in the hospital, in the psych ward. Becky, I think I was your sole source of food. You could drink from a cup but you didn't really eat any solid food. Grandma Rimpel tried bottles, but after my two-week stay in the hospital, I just gave you juice and milk in a cup.

Josh, you said we did things backwards. Well, it worked! It's still working!! I wish Dad was around more, but if he was here, I wouldn't have been able to write to you guys.

So, now you know why Dad might be concerned about you getting serious and how much he wants to be informed. Rest assured that you are all in our prayers. God bless you!

Love,
Mom

---

7 p.m.

PS Our first anniversary was a winner. Dad was going to take me out to dinner, but decided to go to a meeting instead. I was upset and, Josh, you wouldn't stop crying! I went to my friend's house and she took you and you fell right to sleep in her arms. Now I felt like I had a lousy husband and I was a lousy mom! Our friends were on deck to babysit for us. Oh, well...

February 6, 2003
1:20 p.m.

Dear Joshua and Rachel,

I am bursting with joy at your news! First of all, I was really surprised because I really didn't think you could possibly have money to buy a ring, Josh. I am really proud of the way you've saved and have the whole ring already paid for. That is just plain good stewardship and you will be blessed in your whole marriage by continuing to be good stewards of God's abundant blessings. You will see this as one prayer I've listed on my list of Prayers for Kids (PFK's)

Secondly, I feel urged to ask you to review the dating rules I've asked you to follow. They are in effect until your wedding night. Have you ever shared them with Rachel? I was told that being engaged was just like being married in God's eyes and I would agree to some extent, but not when it comes to physically expressing your love for each other. One of the best choices I ever made was to spend the summer before our wedding in Boston, away from Dad. It was one of the hardest things I've ever done, but one of the best.

Thirdly, I know Dad has encouraged you to discuss with each other how many kids you want. That is good advice, but remember that God is in control. We like to think we have a say, but we really don't. It is my earnest prayer that God would bless your marriage with children in due time, but you'll notice on the PFK's that there are three other things that I pray for in your spouse first. I pray that prayer for a spouse twice as much as any other prayer on the list. I try to choose one prayer each day. I started this prayer list when we went to the Grand Canyon. You may remember that that is when I started to cross stitch those prayer requests on a sampler. I finally finished the sampler and had it framed in 2001. It hangs in our computer room. In regard to planning your family, I take a great deal of comfort in knowing that our baby was no surprise to our Heavenly Father.

I'll close now, but I think I'll include the song that I sang at the Labor Day retreat by Turkey Run, the one hosted by Divine Savior of Indianapolis. I truly felt I was telling everyone with my song that I was content with my two kids. All I can figure is that a bunch of people from there started praying for me. How else could this child ever have come to be? The song was initially done by Joni Tada, the quadriplegic, but I rewrote some of the words to tell my story. I did this when I planned a ceremony to renew our vows and I sang it for Dad. You kids were there too. But that was a long time ago. That was when we started using Natural Family Planning. The weak link with us was that I, who have always wanted more kids, was left solely responsible for keeping and interpreting the chart. I can look back now and say, "Here's where we goofed!" But, as I said earlier, I take comfort in knowing that this child is no surprise to our Heavenly Father.

God bless you both. You continue to be in our prayers.

"He who finds a wife finds something good and has obtained favor from the Lord." (Prov. 18:22 NET)

Loads of love,
Mom Rimpel

January 6, 2004 1:20 pm

Dear Brent and Rebekah,

I am just thrilled over your engagement! I wasn't really surprised, except that I don't know how you ever saved enough to buy a ring, Brent. That is just plain good stewardship and you will be blessed in your whole marriage by continuing to be good stewards of God's abundant blessings. You will see this as one prayer I listed on my Prayers for Kids (PFK's)

Secondly, I want to ask you to review the dating rules Becky was asked to give you before your first date when she was in 8th grade. I was told that being engaged was just like being married in God's eyes and I would agree to some extent, but not when it comes to physically expressing your love for each other. One of the best choices I ever made was to spend the summer before our wedding in Boston, away from Dad. It was one of the hardest things I've ever done, but one of the best.

Thirdly, I know Dad encouraged Josh and Rachel, and he probably will encourage you two also, to discuss with each other how many kids you want. That is good advice, but remember that God is in control. We like to think we have a say, but we really don't. It is my earnest prayer that God would bless your marriage with children in due time, but there are three other things I pray for in your spouse first. I pray that prayer for a spouse twice as much as any other prayer on the list. I try to choose one prayer a day, though I haven't been as faithful as I'd like lately. I started this prayer list when we went to the Grand Canyon. You may remember that that is when I started to cross stitch those prayer requests on a sampler. I finally finished the sampler and had it framed in 2001. It hangs down in our study. In regard to planning your family, I take a great deal of comfort in knowing that Jacob was no surprise to our Heavenly Father.

I'll close now, but I think I'll include the song that I sang at the Labor Day retreat by Turkey Run, the one hosted by Divine Savior of Indianapolis. I truly felt I was telling everyone with my song that I was content with my two kids. All I can figure is that a bunch of people from there started praying for me. How else could this little boy ever have come to be? (I also sang this song at the shower for Jacob.) The song was initially done by Joni Tada, the quadriplegic, but I rewrote some of the words to tell my story. I did this when I planned a ceremony to renew our vows and I sang it for Dad. You kids were there too. But that was a long time ago. That was when we started using Natural Family Planning. The weak link with us was that I, who have always wanted more kids, was left solely responsible for keeping and interpreting the chart. I can look back now and say, "Here's where we goofed!" But as I said earlier, I take great comfort in knowing that Jacob is no surprise to our Heavenly Father.

God bless you both. You continue to be in our prayers.

Proverbs 18:22, "He who finds a wife finds something good and has obtained favor from the Lord." (NET)

Love,
Mom Rimpel

CORRESPONDENCE CONTINUED

February 2012

To my Pastor,

"If someone calls your office to talk to you, that automatically puts you in the position of being a listener." (H. Curtis Lyon, "Counseling at the Cross", p. 121)

I think that is the only reason I called to talk to you. I was crushed when you asked, "What do you want me to do?" But that was then and this is now.

I did go back to my psychiatrist as advised by my family doctor. I was discouraged after keeping a log for about two months as to how I was sleeping. He told me my bedtime medicine was enough. I was telling him it wasn't, that there were too many nights I still had lots of trouble sleeping. He said, "What do you want me to do?" I think it was then that he prescribed a sleeping pill, Xanax, to take as needed.

So I went to see Pastor, because I was afraid to take the sleeping pills since I already have trouble getting up in the morning. Also, because Tim said they can be addictive. But my psychiatrist said I have a low dose and I don't have to worry about that. Pastor suggested that I take my sleeping aids EVERY night and not wait to try to fall asleep. So, I try to remember my zyprexa at 8:30 and an hour later I take my sleep aids, melatonin and Gentle Sleep Formula. That was working nicely for a long time.

Then work started to interfere with my sleep as well as my digestive system (I had to make sure a plunger was near!). I have thirty band students to pick solos for, which took me about 3 ½ hours, and I had some idea what I was doing!! I had to get rid of them. I handed them all out that week and finally had some relief. I was able to sleep for about a week, still taking sleep aids nightly, and I started eating prunes every morning.

It is now February. I signed Tim and I up to go to a workshop sponsored by Thrivent on Identity Theft. We were going for hors'd'vours, and I suggested that since we had a sitter, (it was Wednesday night-we skipped choir), that we do something after the meeting was over. We went to Scrementi's, and they served a full-fledged meal! I prayed that Tim would not back out on our date. The meeting was about two hours long, only because we had a meal. The presentation itself was about an hour. After that we went to Dunkin' Donuts. Tim ordered coffee and I had hot chocolate.

I wanted to share with Tim the prayer I'd been praying for him from Stormie Omartian's book, "The Power of a Praying Wife." I read him one, without my glasses, which helped keep me from showing too much emotion or I couldn't see the little print, about his job. (I forgot my glasses.) Anyway the part I shared was something like: help my husband to excel at his work, but free him from the pressure to do so. The prayer was one page long, in contrast to the first prayer in the book that is three pages long. Tim said, "That's nice."

*I also told Tim that I am struggling with discomfort physically between us. I was told when I was first on medicine that this could be a side effect. Having gone through menopause isn't helping either. My psychiatrist said I need estrogen. (more on that later) I'm willing to work on it but so often he just turns his back on me to go to sleep-no goodnight kiss, even. *

Bedtime is my quiet time. Tim reads in the morning long before I know it is a new day. I told Tim that he can interrupt me, and I'll finish up my Bible reading routine later. But almost every night he just turns his back on me. And then when I try to go to sleep he starts snoring or at least breathing very heavily. Sighhhhhh…

The Identity Theft workshop was on February 8th, a Wednesday night. I was really happy to have Tim all to myself. On Valentine's Day, Tim wrote me a note, "I love you!" I read it all day after work. No flowers, no candy (I don't want them), but when he turned his back on me that night... *

Pastor and his wife did a workshop on Gary Chapman's "Five Love Languages." It was great! I don't think Tim knows what mine is. As we walked in , we were asked to tell our spouse's love language, and he didn't remember. Mine is "quality time" and his is "words of affirmation."

Besides working from 9:00 to 2:00 Monday through Thursday, I play for church about twice a month. I try really hard to cook good meals (the way to a man's heart is through his stomach??) I don't even know what else I do. What I don't do well is keep my house in order. EVERY room is a mess, in need of much work, except my studio, my upstairs living room that houses my piano and organ (and no TV!) The only problem there is that you can write in the dust!. One day, a bit ago, Tim was very frazzled from over-working, I think, and was complaining and, etc., so I told him to go back to school! Not very affirmative was I? I apologized for that comment at Dunkin Donuts.

I bought an elliptical machine with some of my dad's inheritance money. Tim asked when I was going to get rid of it because I never used it. So, now I try to use it every day. Just one more thing to do. But I enjoy listening to my favorite radio station while I "walk." It's on my back porch because of my low ceiling in my basement. So I put on my vest and my coat and my stocking cap and my mittens and watched the birds at the neighbors' and...then my foot started to hurt. My machine has eight levels. I only walked for 10 minutes and finally got up to 20 using levels 1,2, and 3 and back to 2 and 1 again.

I not only have bunions on my feet, I have a bunionette on my right foot. The doctor just scraped off the callus. The bunionette is on the outside of my foot by my little toe. $50 to scrape off some calluses. It's only $$. He could do surgery in his office, but neither Tim nor I liked that idea.

Back to my quiet time for just a minute. I write in a college-ruled note-book. I couldn't find a cheap one, so at K-Mart I bought a 5 subject Mead one for $7, only it only cost me $2 because I used our reward points. I was so excited, thinking I'd be set for the rest of my life, but Tim complained about buying paper. * (In his defense, I do have a lot of paper!!)

I go to Curves every chance I get. I can't go in the morning anymore, because Jacob gets picked up at 8:45, and I start work at 9:20, but I like to get the stage set up for lessons. It's quite a lousy place to teach, but we do the best we can. At the junior high, I teach in the ball room. If it's cold outside, I have to dress in layers, because the stage lights get hot, and the ball room gets warm too.

Perhaps you've heard that Josh's voters voted 18-15 to keep the school open one more year. He was so excited to tell us we could now plan our trip to Texas this summer. Tim won't go over Christmas or Easter break, because he has to drive; he won't fly. So I talked to Tim, and we planned our trip. Next thing, Josh and Rchel are planning to caravan with us back to the Midwest. So Tim asked, "Why are we going to Texas when Texas is coming here?! *

I called the kids right away, practically in tears. I have waited too long to take this vacation. Last summer was wonderful, but I want to see Josh and his family. I may have told you before that Tim's idea of vaca-tion is sitting with a beer and watching TV and eating good meals. I'm sorry, but that's not a vacation for me!! Josh said, "But you'd get to spend time with just us without everyone else being around." I said, "I know!" I told Becky that Dad wants me to get the house cleaned up and that that is a heavy burden on me. She said she hoped that we would come and visit them if they lived far away. She said, "Mom, you're busy too!" Thank you, Becky.

So, why can't I sleep? First, I was excited about my band students' solos. This is when my job at school escalates. Some are already talking about doing duets. It's not until April 23 and 24. That's why I was anxious to get rid of all those solos.

*Second, I am a scarecrow stuffed with emotions--mostly, "It doesn't hurt." But is it not true that the wise person controls his/her emotions? I know it's in Proverbs somewhere. (Prov 29:11b NET)

I have chosen this method of communication because you can LISTEN at your leisure. Or, you may choose not to listen at all. At any rate, Pastor comes back from Florida next week, and I hope to go and talk to him yet again and ask if he would be willing to talk to Tim and me. He made a comment to me that if he would have known then what he knows now, he would have done things differently, but he didn't remember saying that.

One more thing, perhaps it's not even necessary to ask. I have no way to communicate with you except by snail-mail. When I call, I talk to Ann and that's fine. I like to talk to Ann. I don't have a working email for you and that's fine too. But I would ask that you would keep Tim and me in your prayers. I am afraid to tell Tim I want to talk to Pastor with him. He'll ask why. I wonder, how do I tell him all this, and will it really make a difference anyway?

May God richly bless you and yours.

Luann

*Things I was stuffing inside.

My psychiatrist told me I needed estrogen, but three reliable friends said, "No, no, and no! Don't take estrogen!!"

Why?

1) Estrogen can increase the risk of breast cancer.
2) Estrogen can cause bone density loss. This is more of a risk for women.
3) Estrogen can cause a greater risk of heart disease.

In 2019, when I asked my chiropractor, she researched some products from Japan and encouraged me to try them. My discomfort is probably due largely to the medications I must take to "keep my head on straight." We're still experimenting, but I feel much better knowing I'm not getting the side effects from taking estrogen.

———

Before Easter 2012

Proverbs 27:10, "Do not abandon your friend or your father's friend; do not go to your brother's home when you are in trouble; a neighbor living nearby is better than a brother far away." (NET)

To my Pastor,

We did get together with Pastor a while back. My printer ran out of ink, and I wanted to type this so it is legible. Pastor asked why I wanted to get together and I told him, "Because Tim is NOT the reason I can't fall asleep. It's not his fault. I am perfectly capable of being unable to fall asleep by myself!"

Tim did remember my love language. I then proceeded to ask him what he remembered from our date at Dunkin Donuts. He had trouble coming up with anything. I reminded him about Stormie's prayer, which he said he did remember. I asked him if we as a married couple are yoked together, why does it so often feel like we are going in opposite directions and working against each other instead of as a team.

I told them about the things I was stuffing, and Pastor said I sounded like an emotional pressure cooker. I started to cry when I told him Tim turned his back on me on Valentine's night. Pastor wanted to know what happens when I blow up.

I lose my appetite and forget to take my medicine and vitamins--but not for long--that would be foolish!

I asked Tim if he would ever kiss me if I didn't catch him as he walked out the door to go back to work after supper.

I told them I prayed a lot and that I felt my prayers were hindered for Tim. Tim said to look up 1 Peter 3. Somehow they felt that the prayers I pray for Tim have already been answered. Pastor said to talk to Tim, that he is a good listener. But I don't think he is a good listener. Nothing seems different since our talk with Pastor. You've probably heard that he is retiring at the end of June. Then what should I do when I can't handle the pressure anymore?

I hardly slept a wink last night. I don't know why. Jacob was up at 3:00 a.m. again. I went from the comfy bed to the couch downstairs, and back to bed with Jacob and back to the couch...and when I weighed in at Curves this morning, I had lost three pounds! What a way to lose weight. NO THANKS!

I am attending a women's Bible class on the book, "Made to Crave," by Lysa Terkeurst. There's lots of optional homework, but I've tried valiantly to keep up. It's really been challenging and fun. Basically, the point is that we are made to crave God, not food.
The owner of Curves suggested that I see a nutritionist since there may be some chemical issues that interfere with my sleep. I better go call, and if I have time I'll walk this to the post office. It is almost 2:30 and I have a lesson at 3:15, but I think I missed the mailman. I guess it was warmer here than in Florida. Crazy, huh? I love it!

Have a blessed Easter,

Luann

August 15, 2012

Dear Pastor and Ann,

I've been meaning to write since your anniversary, but I haven't had a chance until now. I was thinking of you! I decided not to call because I figured you had enough children that would be trying to reach you. I hope you had fun celebrating.

I wanted to tell you that I went back to the nutrition center that started me on my vitamin therapy. I am using their formula now instead of trying to use whatever Shaklee products I can. This way I have a few less pills to swallow. Some are large, some not so much, but most are white. I'm still getting used to counting them out. Some of them I didn't start right away; I still have one to start in September. This is the one I'm a bit nervous about because the nurse told me to start it slow as it could cause some of my former symptoms. When I questioned her on that, the one thing I remember that she said was that I could have some mania. That's scary! She said if I can just make it through the first six weeks I should notice great improvement in my health. I'm supposed to start it in the middle of September. I start work August 27, so at least I'll be used to my new schedule.

In addition to starting these new supplements, many of which are the same, I am on a dairy-free, soy-free, gluten-free diet for two months. Of course, you can't add it all back at once. I'll have to add things back one at a time to see what happens. So far the best thing is that I'm back to pre-Jacob weight!

We just celebrated my little brother's 50th birthday. I tried to think of something really special to give him. I had diaries of all the trips my family took when I was growing up. There were twelve in all. Two of them were for a month, but most were for two weeks. We mostly went to Florida at Christmas and Easter. I typed them all for him. It sure was fun remembering!

The day after my brother's birthday was my nephew's wedding. Both of these were celebrated in Watertown, so we were able to stay with Becky. I did not follow my diet at the wedding reception. I was OK afterward, but I'm doing my best to follow it again until September 8th. I think the first thing I'll add is butter, since another diet said that was the only dairy product I could have.

Please, pray that my medicine prevents any manic symptoms. I will make sure Tim is aware too, as well as our prayer warriors at church (without being too specific.) My psychiatrist thinks the vitamins are "goofy" and all I need is his medicine. I pray his medicine works for those six weeks.

That's all for now. God bless you and yours,

Luann

To my pastor,

Once again, I am opting to use snail-mail to contact you for two reasons. First, Margaret said that you sounded very weak and out of breath. I don't think I can handle hearing you that way. Secondly, I don't want to get in the way of your children who want to check up on you. I will trust Margaret and Becky to keep me informed.

I am keeping you close in prayer, you and your family.

I am hoping this paper isn't too heavy to hold up. If it is, that's OK; it's not that important. I am also sending you a letter I wrote to the nurse at the nutrition center, the place that is ordering my new supplement program. You may find it interesting, or you may not.

I have started that newest supplement. I had asked Tim to "keep an eye on me," as I could struggle for the next six weeks, now closer to four. It seems he is gone even more now. Pastor said he was a good listener. I'm trying to figure out how to approach him without being negative. If this formula works, it should help me sleep better and decrease anxiety and nervousness-good things for me, right? Tim is concerned about the money. I am too, but more than anything, I desperately want to see improvement. I think I will. If it works as well as this diet has, I should be in good shape. I was told I'd need to take the whole bottle before really knowing the results.

I'm praying you'll be able to return to your pulpit and your Bible class as God wills.

God bless you and yours,

Luann

PS If you get to heaven before me, say "hi" to my mom and dad!

September 14, 2012

Dear Maizie,

Wednesday was my 55th birthday. NO BIG DEAL, right? I didn't think it was, anyway.

Tim wrote out a card that had no envelope, but it had a personal note that made it special. Later I found out he had taken one from my card box. No big deal.

At work, many students wished me "Happy Birthday." Even Tim came to where I teach and wished me the same. I was feeling pretty good.

After I got Jacob off the bus, I packed the car with my folder for my meeting at church, the diaper bag, our choir folders, and my music to practice for church since I play on Sunday. I also remembered the Subway card and some extra cash. All during my meeting I was thinking of that wonderful chicken salad. I had written a note to Tim with what to put on my salad, you know-spinach too, oil and vinegar, salt and pepper and vinegar, I never even thought to list ALL the vegetables. I had a terrible thought. Would he remember that I couldn't eat a sandwich? He did remember! But when I opened my salad, something looked different. I realized there were no vegetables on my salad, just lettuce and spinach.

I was crushed, to say the least. I told him I just wanted to cry. He asked if I wanted his sandwich, which I couldn't eat. My whole day was ruined at this point. I wondered how long it would take to recover my stability. Tim went home to get some bean salad with a dressing I can eat and I ate that with my salad.

Then I went to Curves. A lady, whom I only met once, had a card waiting for me. I started to feel better. They sang "Happy Birthday" to me.

After Curves I went to church to practice if I could. When I walked in, some friends were waiting and sang "Happy Birthday" and I got two hugs.

I went to choir practice and they sang "Happy Birthday" in harmony! I have never in my life had that happen before. I almost started to cry. Tim got there ten minutes later.

Jacob was singing to me after school. I didn't understand all the words, but "at the cross," came out very clear. He kept singing it over and over and over.

When we got home from choir, I had to practice, so I asked Tim to put Jacob to bed. One of his buddies from church called for him, and I answered and asked if Tim could call him back after Jacob was in bed. Tim spent the rest of the evening talking to him, and I didn't even see him until the next day. I don't think it's an exaggeration to say he spent more time with his buddy than with me.

Yesterday, I got a card from Tim's sister. Guess what she gave me? A $10 Subway card! I don't think she'll ever know how much that meant to me.

But, I'm telling you all this because I have a question. How am I supposed to maintain stability with so many ups and downs? And yet, here I am, doing just fine two days later.

Thanks, Maizie. I'll call after a little more time on my new program. So far, so good.

God bless you and yours,

Luann

Maizie was a nurse at the nutrition center where I got my supplements.

This was my schedule before Holy Week 2013:

3/22   Friday afternoon I went to see, "Pinocchio", by the Children's Theater; Friday evening we went to visit a friend in Lowell and see the play, "Grease."
3/23   I hosted a table for our Lenten Tea and we watched Audrey's drama on Christ's Passion. There was a funeral in there somewhere. That night the junior high did the comedy, "The Frog Prince of Spamalot"
3/24   Sunday night was the ILHS Sacred Concert.

This was a lot of stimulation.

These were the things on my "to do" list

Write letter
Do dishes
Five loads of laundry

Count out my supplements
Practice for church

I had to write to my pastor first; then I got everything else done. But that's when I decided that maybe I wasn't as OK as I thought!

3/24/2013

Dear Pastor, my pastor,

It's me again. Margaret told me at church today that you are going to retire. God's richest blessings on that decision.

I have a list, but I only have a little time.

For about two weeks, I was getting eight to nine hours of sleep/night and not needing any extra help. I should have known something was brewing. Of late, I needed half of a xanax for about a week, and now I just take a whole tablet when I go to bed. Going to bed is my least favorite thing to do. I love our tempurpedic mattress, and I love my husband. I'm just scared I won't fall asleep without help, which means I'll have trouble getting up in the morning.

Why?

1. I was a hostess for our Lenten Reflections brunch, so I had to set a table for seven. But I had invited six Catholic neighbors, one Christian Reformed, and one Zion member, and they were all coming! I needed two tables, but I could hardly host one. One of my friends hosted a table with all my neighbors from this side of the tracks. After the brunch, we went into the sanctuary to watch a drama that Audrey wrote about women of the Passion. It was wonderful. Very moving.

So, why was this a problem? I was SO EXCITED they were all coming and to use my good China, BUT I needed a table cloth. Our round tables at church are 72" in diameter. K Mart didn't have one that worked, nor did Kohls. I went to get Tim and he took me to Tuesday Morning, and they sent us to Bed, Bath and Beyond. We did find a suitable one there. I also bought napkins and a pitcher. Now I had to find time to iron the silly thing. Ever since I ironed a hole in my sister's bridesmaid dress, I have had a phobia of ironing. But I did it, and my table looked very nice.

2. I play organ for church Maundy Thursday, keyboard for Easter Sunday and organ for the Sunday after Easter. I just found that out. I have to have the keyboard music ready by Tuesday to practice with the singers, because it's Holy Week. One of the songs is really hard with all the repeats. Pray for me, please.

3. I'm planning my spring recital on Mother's Day, because that is the only evening I can rent Zion's fellowship hall. In the midst of all the hustle and bustle, I am also preparing a selection, "La Paloma," by some Spanish composer. It means, "The Dove." It's a piece I worked up in high school, and it's not that hard. It's pretty easy and I enjoy doing it; "it" just doesn't enjoy me!

One of my students is 5 years old. He started taking lessons when he was 2 ½ years old, and now we know he has perfect pitch. We've known that for a while. One of his selections is "Turkish March," and he takes it up to speed. I have to practice the accompaniment that goes with his part. It's a privilege to work with him. But not him alone; I love working with all my students. I think it will be a wonderful way to celebrate Mother's Day.

4. I must still follow a dairy-free, gluten-free, soy-free diet. What a hassle! I have some expensive enzymes to take if I choose to break my diet, so I must choose wisely, or everyone around me will suffer to my embarrassment.

5. My psychiatrist and my OB doctor, who will not be anymore, put me on estrogen. Even though a friend had said, " NO!", I followed the doctor's advice and filled the prescription. When I saw him the next time, I told him, "I hate it!" This time Tim was with me, and neither of us appreciated his advice (OB doctor). In the meantime, I spent $50, and then through the Prime Mail, another $100 for the same amount! Now I'll end up throwing it away! Two more friends said, "No! And No!, don't take estrogen. My nurse practitioner suggested an over-the-counter remedy and that seems to help.

I'm almost done here. At the Tea I talked to other ladies. One had served two Lenten suppers in a row with a Girl Pioneer one in between. One is struggling to get the flowers ready for Easter Sunday. The church secretary asked for prayers for the office. Remember how busy things get? Another wondered if she has diabetes. My point: I am not alone. I'm not the only one struggling this time of year. And I wonder how you're doing.

I received my new supplements in the mail. Now I start counting them out, so I have to figure out how. It should be easy though. It's just that there's "oodles" of dishes, China included, I'm doing laundry, checking on Jacob--he's such a good little boy! One of the subs said, "He's so cute you can't help but smile when he's naughty!" A six month supply of supplements is about $800, and when I did Shaklee it was about $200/month, plus I also went to the Health Food Store a lot. I do have to check in with the supplement doctor annually, which is about $600. That's another thing I have to do: count out my supplements for the week.

The lights just flickered, and there is not a storm! I better hurry. Tim sets out a Bible verse for Jacob and me when he remembers. I like that.

6. My band students, about 30, are preparing solos for May 6 and 7. No big deal? I wish!

I do have a tremor that is a nuisance due to my depakote that I take twice a day. I can still knit and crochet and play piano and organ. But I can't hold my bulletin steady or write letters or 30 band reports without trouble, to say the least. So, I tremble more than a little.

Gotta run. God's blessings on your birthday and may He grant many more.

April 1, 2013

Dear Pastor, my pastor,

I just want to share a few reflections from Holy Week in my heart and at Trinity.

I have hammer toes; Jesus had a hammer drive nails into his hands and feet.

I took a soup mug to school to warm up for my lunch. When I got it out, it looked like someone had decorated the upper edge; it was beautiful. But there was no mess in the microwave. At home I made a big batch of chicken soup and was getting all vegetables and only a little broth. While pouring it into another pot, "my cup overflows," but not too much of a mess!

"Thou preparest a table before me"-I eat my soup for breakfast, lunch and super if I can't find anything else. The meat is a bit soft because instead of three hours, I cooked it for over five because we were at church practicing so long! It slides down easily. I use sorghum bread crumbs for croutons because that's all I have left. Now I have to bake more bread. My recipe uses a bunch of different flours from the health food store.

I just ordered new glasses. Tim got his new pair last month, but I planned to order supplements, so I decided to wait on my glasses. I didn't want to overload the credit card. Tim takes his glasses off to read anyway! I just want to see my notes clearer. I ordered prescription sunglasses and anti-glare. Moses used a veil. My glasses cost over $400! And that was without the exam because the ophthalmologist, who treats me for glaucoma, had already written the prescription.

Maundy Thursday night I did not sleep at all. I only knew that because I never woke up. I was not watching the clock; my thoughts were not racing. I just didn't fall asleep. Jesus didn't sleep on Maundy Thursday either! But I didn't think about that. I knew I had nothing to do that took clear thinking on Good Friday. "He makes me lie down in green pastures." We took our time between services on Maundy Thursday and got Subway for supper. I was thinking church started at 7:30 and realized at 6:42 that I was not going to be able to play my 15 min of pre-service. No longer did I fear being so relaxed that I would miscount verses. Tyler rang the bells for the start of church and during the Lord's Prayer, and he subtracted a couple stops so the organ would not overpower the choir. That was Tim's job, but he never made it.

Good Friday I went to my prayer meeting with Jacob, because Tim was going to Kankakee to get an ID to get into the Detention Center and eventually be able to speak to the prisoners there. Jesus went to prison. (1 Peter 3:19) We finished at the same time. Jacob ate Cheerios while we prayed. I had a massage (that wasn't like Jesus), went to church to take communion at 3:30 , and choir sang at 6:00 and 7:00 for the Tenebrae services. I was sad, more than sad, that my friend and her sister didn't come. I don't know if they'll come for Easter and they didn't come Christmas Eve or Day either. I am concerned that my friend's granddaughter has not been baptized.

I slept well Friday night; "He restoreth my soul."

I've been awfully thirsty because of the extra sleep medicine I've been taking. "I thirst." I did not take anything to help me sleep on Maundy Thursday and Good Friday. I hope I don't need help tonight. I have a lot of notes to play tomorrow. Thanks so much for your prayers.

Stevie and his little brother came to our Easter egg hunt at Trinity. There was a puppet show with an Easter bunny singing about Jesus!!! Stevie's mom asked if we had church services on Easter Sunday, and I replied, "Church on Easter Sunday? OF COURSE we have church!" She told me her church doesn't have services on Easter Sunday. I think they will come. That makes me somewhat nervous because Stevie may be able to hear me miss my octaves!! (He's the student that's 5 years old and has perfect pitch.)

I had another thought, but I lost it, and I need to give Jacob a bath so we can go shopping to use my 30% off at Kohls and my 25% at Carsons. Tim is not happy for me to look at new clothes. He wants me to get rid of clothes. I truly don't wear many dresses because of the special shoes I must wear. I even wear dresses with my tennis shoes to teach at school.

I may call after you get this letter.

Thanks for listening.

Love,
Luann

PS All this "stuff" I've been sharing: Is it a cross I have to bear, or a thorn in my flesh?

June 20, 2013
(Thank you note from my pastor)

Dear Tim and Luann,

It was wonderful to see you Sunday. I want to thank you for being there and for your kind gift.

God bless you all now and in the years to come.

Yours in Christ,
Curt

(We met Pastor and his family in Wisconsin to celebrate his retirement from the ministry before we went to Camp BASIC.)

July 2013

Dear Pastor and Ann,

I hope it's OK if I still call you Pastor. I can't think of you any other way. Happy Anniversary!

I wanted to share a couple things, so I thought I'd quickly send a note. I'm supposed to be getting ready to go to Becky's, but that shouldn't take long. Tim's mom and sister are coming to Crete tomorrow morning; we are going out to breakfast and then to Becky's. Josh and his family will be there too. A good time will be had by all! I keep praying for safe travels. My sister, Lorna, and her husband are going to come and see everyone too. I should still call Linda so she doesn't feel left out. (She had hip replacement surgery June 3rd.)

Pastor, when I talked to you on the phone, I was greatly encouraged to be reminded that all Christians face persecution from those that are invisible. I don't feel so alone in my struggle. My illness(es) are definitely a thorn in my flesh.

One more thing I quickly wanted to share were the scripture verses I use for my Quiet Time. I write down notes in a notebook: date, time, hymn, Bible reading, prayers... Anyway, at the top of my notebook is "LORD, help.." Then I write down several Bible verses. The first one I write is Psalm 46:10 (NIV), "Be still...:" That's when I think of you, Ann. On the other side I write, Proverbs 2:7a (NIV), "He holds victory...[in store for the upright]" In the middle right under "LORD, help…", I write Mark 6:31b (NIV), "Come with me…[by yourselves to a quiet place and get some rest.]" Those are the ones I've used for years.

Just recently I added three more verses. I am constantly losing/misplacing things. It is a daily occurence in my life!" I thought of, "You have not…[because you ask not.]" Tim told me that was James 4:2c. I always told the kids to pray when they lost something (wallet or purse, etc.) because Jesus knew where it was. On the other side, I write, "I will yet praise him, [my Savior and my God.]" (NIV) I was thrilled to find that verse of praise three times in Psalms 42 and 43. Finally, in the middle, I write another verse Tim shared from our Bread Basket of Bible verses: "Before they call, [I will answer.]" (Isaiah 65:24 NIV) The header of my Quiet Time is pretty full, but it's full of wonderful promises.

God bless you two, and I look forward to hearing from you at Christmastime as you are able.

People keep asking me if you are still in Wisconsin. I just tell them I don't know.

God bless you and yours,
Tim, Luann and Jacob

———————————

Notes to talk to Lori

Joy, Joe, Caroline, Agnes, Rose-elderly who need care (Today they are all in heaven.)

Bible class: Sunday morning, Monday night, Wednesday morning and Thursday night-too much

Playing for church: keyboard on October 6-two songs had four sharps and went fast, plus I had to remember to transpose up a half step to +1 and back down to 0; organ October 13-keeping it simple. I played "Let

Us Ever Walk With Jesus" with Tim on trumpet. (Tim didn't share my enthusiasm. This hymn was sung at my wedding.)

Sunday's recognition of called workers-we'll have company-Yes, Tim's sister is planning to come and she wants to stay for the presentation on the gay life style Sunday night

I've been needing half a sleeping pill for over a week now. That makes me very thirsty. But I was doing so well before that!

Cooking, practicing, keeping an eye on Jacob though he's out of diapers and pull-ups he has many accidents and I feel it's my fault for not watching the clock

I haven't sent a card to Helen or Dawn or Rich and Judy

Because I am so thirsty and I take so many supplements I have to drink lots of water, but it's hard to find time to go to the bathroom! I'm up at least once every night.

Tim really likes to listen to a couple radio shows: Janet Parshal-The Market Place of Ideas and Julie Roys-Up For Debate, but he doesn't, at least I don't think he likes to listen to me. All I do is complain and ask him for more help.

(This was the list I took to talk to Lori. The February 15, 2015 letter was the result.)

February 15, 2015

Can you guess why I'm writing? I'll tell you. I'm on a rollercoaster ride. I know you know what I mean.

It all started that fateful day of Dec 13 when I went to get a haircut. I turned down a side street and heard a crack like a big stick breaking. But there was no stick! I looked back and was horrified to see the driver's side view mirror hanging on the car I'd just passed. I got my haircut and came back to investigate the scene of the crime. It was true! I panicked and ran. Hit and run. I never thought to see if there was any damage to my mirror. There wasn't.

We went to Florida to see Josh and his family over Christmas break. We had a wonderful time.

Rachel kept us well-fed. I know I gained weight-no Curves, good food and lots of rest.

We came home and I read in Meditations about Samuel: "Speak, Lord, your servant is listening." When I do my quiet time, that's the last thing I write. It seemed the Lord wanted me to confess my sin. I chose to tell the Pastor and he said to go to the police and be honest. The officer checked three times and could find no reports of vandalism. Basically, I was off the hook.

Except I had to tell Tim. I waited until he was driving and he didn't get upset. "Thank you, Jesus."

That was a loop-de-loop that went upside down and around a few times.

Do you remember my sister that called you once? Her daughter is pregnant. I was glad to hear she knew who the father was. My niece won't talk to her mother at all. This is really a low dip.

I went to the post office to mail some pictures of Jesus with children of all ages to my niece, in care of her parents, and there was this lady in the lobby with a blanket. I had to ask what on earth she was doing with her baby. I was trying to get to Curves by 4:30, and I had to drop Jacob off at ILHS. The lady was trying to fit a large blanket in a small box to mail to her daughter in Japan. I said, "Let's pretend we're camping and we have to fit our tent in this duffle bag." She took one end and I took the other; we folded and rolled, and guess what? It fit perfectly! I said, "God bless you," and hurried on my way. For some reason, Jacob sat on a chair while we folded. This was a high peak.

I play for church Ash Wed, March 4, and Maundy Thur. I don't think I'll have much trouble, but I think that is the reason for the quivers in my insides. I've had the service lay-outs for over two weeks, I think. I've started, but I have more work to do. Ash Wed is a big service. For offertory I plan to play a song Josh wrote with a high school girl singing. Now to find time to get together...Mar 4 the MLC choir will be here, but I must prepare preservice, offertory and post-service music. That's nerve-wracking with all those good musicians! And Maundy Thur is a big service too. "Dear Lord, all to Your glory and not to mine. Amen"

I've been forgetting some things. One day, I didn't take any supplements and it was after supper. I decided it was too late to make them up, so I declared a fast and took only my medicine. A couple times I took my supper supplements at bedtime-not good. I have to remind myself to take a shower and wash my hair.

Monday night small group Bible study has been just Debi and me. It's really been nice. We miss the others, but the one-on-one has been priceless. I've been coasting back and forth a bit getting ready for a big hill. Ready? Here it comes:

In July, my brother, the poet, is taking me to Boston to visit the family I worked for the summer before I married Tim. It is my fervent prayer that I get to see them all again. Mr. N is having hip surgery, or may be recovering by this time. Mrs. N has a birthday soon, so I will send her a card. After that summer , I remembered all their birthdays as best I was able. I was hired to work with their son, David. I think David is a Christian. We sang "Jesus Loves Me" to him every night when we gave him his bath. He lives really close by, so I should be able to see them all, IF I can just get out there with my head on straight. The family is Jewish. Mrs. N offered us a place to stay at their house when we come. I think they are 88 and 90 years old. Please pray for me.

The ride is almost over.

I've opted to miss a ministry leader's meeting at church to go to a handbell workshop. The Agape Ringers are wonderful! Their 20 minute concert is worth $35 alone. Tim has Bible class to prepare for and he'll have Jacob all day. It's Saturday and I'll be home for supper.

When we moved from Park St, I packed four boxes of STUFF to sort. I finally did so because we had three snow days in a row. Or should I say, "cold days?" I sorted and sorted and sorted. I read and read and read. I found things for Josh and Becky and things like the pictures of Jesus I sent to my niece. It was a slow process. I ended up being up too late a couple nights, and I couldn't go to sleep. I felt overwhelmed with blessings.

Normally I have a pretty good appetite. Lowell sent me a box of cheeses for Christmas: one spread, two blocks and some mustard. I ate almost all the cheese myself! And what do you eat with cheese? Rice cakes and corn tortillas didn't always grab me. And what was in the mustard? Soy! So much for my dairy-free, soy-free, gluten-free diet!! I was having some trouble in the bathroom, so I increased my fruits and, well, veggies never were much trouble. I snack on sunflower seeds without salt and mixed nuts. The next can of nuts will be salt-free. Why? Tim is concerned about his blood pressure.

Anyway, I have to remind myself to eat. And lately I can't get to the bathroom soon enough!

I find myself talking to myself as I go about my tasks each day. I'm warning myself, "Your thoughts are racing; slow down!" Getting off--

Jacob made it to the top of the list for free one-on-one swimming lessons with the Special Olympics. The problem is that they are on Tuesday in Lansing. Tuesday is Prison Ministry night for Tim. I told Tim, "There are other men who can go to the prison, but Jacob has only one dad." Tim does not want me driving to TF South in the dark, or in the light, for that matter. It was on the way home that I told him about my hit and run.

I talked to Lori, and she encouraged me not to beat myself up anymore. She reminded me that the devil likes to keep us in the pit. We talked for over an hour. She is such a blessing to our church!

I just want you to know that I have a ton of dishes in the sink. I made chili-mac for a friend with leukemia yesterday. After my prayer meeting this morning I decided to skip Curves. (My jitters should probably give me extra muscle tone!) I skipped organ practice. (It's Friday and I always take off on Friday. But I think I'll try to find some preservice music AFTER I do the dishes and EAT something more!) It was more important to me that I get this written.

God bless you and yours,
Luann

———————————

March 22, 2017

Dear Pastor Lyon,

I don't have much time, so I'll be brief. I have a birthday card to send and figured I could send a note as well. I hope you have a wonderful birthday.

I was kind of dumb-founded when you said you didn't know you were supposed to reply to any of my correspondence. Forgive me for assuming that since Ann told me she didn't write letters, I thought you wouldn't either. I didn't want you to feel you had to reply, so I usually asked you to just listen. Maybe it was every letter I wrote. At any rate, I would gladly receive a reply when and if you ever have time.

My concern, as I think I've told you before, is that it really helps to write to you when I'm struggling. You've confirmed that so often it relates to my commitments at church, especially when I play for festival services. I just wonder what I should do if you are not there to write to. I thought I was done grieving your loss when you left Crete, but now I know I will struggle if you go to heaven before me. Do you have any suggestions? I am open.

We talked on New Year's Eve for about a half hour and I forgot to ask you about my struggle with food. There was a challenge at Curves and my goal was to get to the next lowest notch on the scale, to the tune of losing about five pounds. I met the challenge and won a shirt as did five other gals. I've been trying to find other sins to confess, because it seems that using gluttony as my sin of choice is preventing me from taking note of other sins I should be confessing.

We had a Bible class on a book by Beth Moore called "Living Free." We learned to pray Scripture. Our assignment, now that class is over, is to pray through the Psalms. In this class we were asked to list our sins. I went to work and I had a list on my index card and I was going to be ready when I got to the "confessing of my sins" part of my Quiet Time routine. Then she told us to tear it up! I did, but I tucked it away in the back of my book so I could put it together at some later date. She went on to assure us that all our sins are forgiven and forgotten by God. So when I got home, I recycled it...

Tim is teaching Apologetics 101 on Sunday mornings. Because I've been playing mostly organ, I've been able to attend his class. I've really enjoyed that! He puts SO much time into preparing. He already taught this class to the men on Wednesday mornings, so he is just re-doing it, which is not nearly the preparation time it took him to prepare for it initially.

If you feel you have any words of wisdom to share, I would love to hear from you. There's no rush.

God bless you and yours,
Luann

(This letter is before Pastor's reply from Victorville-he replied to this letter)

———————

St. John Lutheran Church
16700 Green Tree Blvd.
Victorville, CA 92395
760-245-9090

Dear Luann,

Thanks for the birthday greetings and for writing. I thought I would write back just to prove I sometimes do. I'm happy to hear about all the things you're doing and hope they all continue to go well.

You talked a lot about things you have and do feel guilty about. I would encourage you to focus on the unconditional forgiveness that Christ won for you and for all people. You can't see it much more clearly than you can see it right now during the Lent and Easter season. We all have more sins than we can recall. God knows them. You don't need to enumerate them. If one particular sin bothers you you know that you need to go to the cross and hear Jesus tell you again that it is finished. You will not do yourself any good by looking for things to feel guilty about. The whole idea of idols in our lives is an unending search. The point is not what you choose to idolize, the problem is that all of us have the ability to make idols out of anything. Any time you fear, love, or trust in something more than God it is a sin against the first commandment. We need to look to Christ for the strength to avoid that. The other side of that coin is looking to Christ for the assurance of forgiveness that provides all the motivation you need to put Jesus in the first place he demands and deserves. That would be a better thing to work on. You know that already.

Thanks again for the greetings and the kind letter. Please greet anyone we know and especially the rest of the family.

Yours in Christ,
Curt
H. Curtis Lyon

July 27, 2019

Dear Lori,

Lysa's Bible study this summer was very inspiring and enlightening. I was thoroughly fascinated by this study and wanted to share a few things with you.

You know we have struggled in our marriage. I don't remember the particular struggle, for there were many times I struggled, but I went to my piano lesson and asked my teacher what to do. I told my teacher that I believed the older women were to teach the younger and asked if she had any advice for me. This is what she said: "Love your enemies; do good to those who hurt you." And I thought, 'my husband is my enemy?' And so I tried to love Tim in my hurt. But the concept of him being my enemy stuck.

At the last bullet point on p. 155 in the study guide Lysa asks about disappointments and sufferings. I wrote: I need to turn to Jesus in Tim's absence. That can make me a stronger Christian, providing I stop trying to change him. I need to think of him as my friend, having him become my best friend, rather than my enemy!

On p. 156 at the first bullet point, Lysa asks where we see glimpses of joy in the midst of our hurt. I wrote: Tim calls me much more often, but usually only when he's coming home. I consider each call a joy. Lately, though, he's called several times.

You know, I asked Tim once, who his best friend was. I knew without a shadow of a doubt that it was his college roommate. But I was wrong! He said ME!! I guess our idea of friendship is a little different. He will call Dean and talk to him a LONG time. Tim hardly talks to me at all, usually just in passing or to share info from school or to tell me he is coming home. I talk to Tim EVERY DAY! He hardly ever talks to Dean. I decided I needed to start to consider Tim as my friend. My friends at Mom's Time Out encouraged me to do so.

Still on p. 156, at the second bullet point under #3, she asked us to list comfort from others. I wrote: The suggestion to bless Tim each night was a turning point. "The Lord bless you and keep you; the Lord make his face shine upon you and be gracious to you; the Lord look on you with favor and give you his peace." (Numbers 6:24-26 - NIV) Though Tim is often not in bed with me, when he is, I bless him, just as I recite the blessing over Jacob at bedtime. I realized God could use me to bless Tim, even though I felt so needy.

On p. 161 Lysa asked how this study affected me. I wrote: When I struggle with feeling lonely, like a pig (gluttony), or full of pride, I know this is dust in my life that God can turn into beautiful pottery.

Finally Lysa asked us to write a prayer of restoration. There were three areas in my life that I worked on in this study. I addressed each one in my prayer. I began my prayer with thanksgiving for the many opportunities to read, hear and study God's Word freely and openly. Then I addressed each issue I worked on in this study.

1) The loneliness I have dealt with in my marriage I looked at as dust. God has blessed us with Jacob. Tim is more present and Jacob is a great joy.

2) I was reduced to dust when I was not allowed to play for church for four long years while I struggled with my health. I found a piano and organ teacher and improved my skills. Now I have been restored and I play for church once or twice a month. Praise the Lord!!! This is where I struggle with pride. I always pray that I may play for His glory and not for mine.

3) My driver's license is a lie! My weight is not correct. I don't feel restored in this area and I don't know what to do.* I pray this struggle brings me closer to Jesus, but I also wonder, 'Is this just vanity?' I consider food an idol in my life.

Thank you for letting me share. I loved this study and I learned a lot.

One of the things I found remarkable about the videos was that Lysa shared very little of her personal struggle in them. She pointed us to Jesus.

*When I renewed my license in 2021, I corrected my shrunken height and increased my weight!

Excerpts from letters to Lisa:

3/23/20
On 3/18/20 while preparing a meal for a family that just had a baby, I tripped and fell in my kitchen. I stubbed my toe (shoes on-thank God!) on the bench of our kitchen table and literally flew across my kitchen. There was nothing to catch me. I landed on my L knee cap, rebounded onto my R knee and R elbow and bashed my front teeth on the floor. I was stunned! My knee cap didn't feel broken and my teeth felt whole.

5/4/20
I had a hairline fracture in my L knee cap. I wore a leg brace for a month and got it off 4/30/20. The Lord stopped the whole world so I could heal and Jacob was here to help me because of the pandemic.

Basically, I'm not teaching lessons at school because there is no school; I'm not playing for church because there is no public worship; and I'm not teaching lessons from home. I'm making no $$ and just costing Tim more!

6/1/20
I just became a rep for the Juice Plus Company. I plan to take their products now and hope to replace all or most of what I take from the nutrition center, which could save us money. I want to start soon while I still have some supplements leftover so I can fall back on them if my health begins to fail. I'll actually make $$ as a rep. I'm excited

because I think this will work, but I'm a little scared too. Please keep me in your prayers.

7/1/20
I switched to all Juice Plus and no supplements from the nutrition center. I also use some things from Shaklee. A bone density test revealed that I have osteoporosis! I wonder how that is possible since I've been taking calcium/magnesium all these years.

9/1/20
I started teaching my band lessons yesterday 8/31. I have Jacob's remote lessons, then I teach lessons at school during Jacob's long lunch hour and then we hurry home for more remote lessons. I don't teach band lessons on Tues, but Diana comes one week for flute and the next for piano. I have four remote band lessons at 4:00, 4:30, 5:00 and 5:30. On Wed I teach four lessons at the JH and only three on Thur. It's a lot to keep track of, but I think it will work out ok. Blood tests from my Dr were good. My Curves coach said that my friends thought I was doing well.

10/1/20

I'm used to Jacob's and my schedules. It's been a good month. I got a bunch of tomatoes from a friend at church and made two large kettles of tomato soup all by myself. (I've been eating it from the freezer all by myself too!) But I had also gotten ten 15 oz containers of ricotta cheese from my neighbor, so I made two 9x13" pans of lasagna. The kitchen was a disaster. That was 9/13. The same neighbor gave us a bunch of apples. Jacob and I counted, peeled, cored and sliced 55 apples and I made applesauce on 9/20. With our busy schedules I couldn't do any of this during the week, so I had to do them on Sundays.

11/1/20

On Mon 10/26 it snowed. I told Becky she didn't have to send her snow to us!!

On Tuesday night I was awake all night, unable to sleep at all. In the morning I texted Josh and Becky to pray for me. Becky got right back to me and asked if my meds had changed. I knew right away that that was the trouble. You see, when COVID started back in March and I had fallen, I was not going to school to teach band lessons, or playing for church, or teaching from home. I had NO STRESS-sort of. My Dr and I decided to try two tablets of depakote instead of three. I called her and she called back before we got our coats on to leave. She said she wouldn't change my meds until she talked to me at 6:00 that night. So, I worried that she might not agree that I needed to go back up. Guess what? I have SAD (Seasonal Affective Disorder). Basically, the change of seasons affects me adversely. Know what else? The last two nights there was a full moon. I think that affects me too. I just couldn't handle everything. I am waiting for my new prescription to come. She ordered something to help me sleep too-something non-addictive. (hydroxyzine) So, I started back on three tablets.

I also made an appointment to see Pastor. What joy, comfort and peace that discussion brought.

12/2/20

I saw Pastor twice more and really appreciated his listening ear. Once my new medicine kicked in and I got the needed sleep, I felt much better.

My conclusion is that I do fine with Juice Plus as long as my medicine is regulated properly. I am taking a couple things from the nutrition center and from Shaklee. I liked taking less medicine as I think it helped reduce my "nuisance tremor," but I don't want to deal with NO SLEEP again! The tremor doesn't keep me from knitting, crocheting, or playing piano or organ. It's just a nuisance! I just couldn't handle my stressful schedule on the lower dose of my depakote, which controls the mania end of my bi-polar/manic-depression.

November 17, 2020 5:51 a.m.

Dear Pastor Lyon,

Greetings from Crete, where we wake to frost on our windows and we need to wear jackets to stay warm.

I am struggling of late. In the last two weeks I've awakened twice before 3 a.m. and last night I slept until 11 p.m. and woke up ready to start my day! Yikes!! I just want to sleep until I'm not tired anymore.

The utility bulb in our fridge keeps blinking out, especially if I bump it. I was irritated, but then I remembered the Source of electricity and it's been better ever since. I'm still careful not to bump it.

I'm having trouble telling time. My Activity Tracker tracks my steps/day and my hours (minutes!) of sleep/night. It got out of sync with my cell, so it stayed on Daylight Savings Time. I had to remember which way to adjust the hour. I wore my cross watch too, but it only has four numbers, so it is hard to tell exactly what time it is. I need to know the minutes, so I know when my lessons start and end. I had to check my cell for the exact time. One of my students wasn't sure her lesson was over yet, but I told her that on all three accounts, she was late getting back to class. The student afer her never forgets, so I wasn't watching the time, but she was testing and couldn't come. At church I was practicing at 10 a.m. but the organist's clock read 3 p.m. I took the clock to Pastor, but he was leaving and lef it on the secretary's desk. I did not tell the head organist, and she sent out an all out alert looking for it!

My psychiatrist wants to raise my meds even more if... I will tell her the hydroxyzine she prescribed to help me sleep works, but when I wake up, I can't fall back to sleep. Today is an easy day for me. I teach only remote lessons from 4 to 6.

I think I know what might be part of the problem. Sarah is in the process of editing a manuscript I wrote telling my story of my struggle with manic-depression. About one third is letters I wrote to you afer you left Crete. I don't know if it will ever get published, but I don't intend to list you by name. Let me know if you have any concerns, or if you'd like to see it. Joyce suggested that you might be able to help me, but Sarah has a master's degree in psychology and she's here. She said she was honored to be asked. Besides, she hasn't been able to get a job anywhere. Believe me-she's tried!

I want to go to heaven where there is "no more night." (Revelation 21:25)

Your sister,
Luann

6:24 a.m.
November 25, 2020

Dear Luann,

Thanks for your letter that we received recently. I'm hoping that all the many things that you always seem to be able to keep going are going well. I'm sure that, as always, you are providing many things to many people in service to our Lord.

Among other things you said that you are working on memories of your struggles over the years. You asked if I had any problem with making reference to me in them. I am flattered that you would think of that and I certainly have no objections to using references to me in any way that is helpful. When I asked the same thing of others that I have written or spoken about the answer always came back, "Sure, if it will help someone." That is my answer too.

Tonight we will have a Thanksgiving Eve service outside at 6:30. I am not sure what to expect, but I better get to the final touches for the service. Our pastor took a call to Lake Geneva, WI and I am currently serving as the vacancy pastor.

I wish you, Tim and Jacob, and of course the others, children and grand-children a blessed Thanksgiving and the assurance of the continuing love of Christ as we remember his birth and look forward to a new year.

Yours in Christ,
Rev H Curtis Lyon
Pastor Lyon

Postscript

Tim, my beloved husband, did two things for me that really touched my heart:

1) He hired the high school singers to come and serenade me on Valentine's Day. One song they sang was, "I Can't Help Falling in Love With You." He wanted it to be a surprise but he had to tell me to make sure I would be home. I almost cried, it was so special!

2) For my 60th birthday he wanted to plan a surprise birthday party for me. He didn't know what to do. If he did it in Crete, he had no idea who to invite because we have so many friends, and then, he had no idea how much food he should have. If he did it in MI, it would be for his family, but not for my brothers and sisters. He was stressed, until he thought of Becky! Becky knows how to throw a party!! She sent out invitations, bought special plates, napkins, and cups for the occasion, a bouquet of flowers, balloons, and she even made gluten-free cupcakes for me! It was perfect from top to bottom. On the way home I commented that that was a pretty expensive weekend. He said, "You're worth it!"

I feel very blessed!

Soli Deo Gloria!

Conclusion

If you have been blessed by reading this book, I would love to hear from you. If you have questions or comments about anything in my book, please feel free to contact me at:

luannpunkerimpel@hotmail.com

I will do my best to answer in a timely fashion. In the meantime, I will do my best to pray for you.

God bless you and yours,
Luann (Punke) Rimpel

CPSIA information can be obtained
at www.ICGtesting.com
Printed in the USA
LVHW050255180122
708488LV00009B/262